Don Nori, Sr. has been on a lifelong quest to test and explore the realm of what is possible. In his newest book, *The God Watchers*, he continues to delve deep in the spiritual realm uncovering the undeniable key to living in an atmosphere where truly *all* things *are* possible! My encouragement to you is to read this and become a God Watcher. Then watch *your* life change in ways you never could have imagined!

RONDA RANALLI
Publisher, Destiny Image

Don Nori continues to encourage us to be a people who are after nothing less than knowing and manifesting the heart of God—walking in the dreams of His heart.

MEGAN HAYES
Greensboro, North Carolina

It is so reassuring to hear that what God is awakening in me concerning progressive and corporate revelation is in line with what the spirit is saying to the church!

MARTIE SMIT
Port Nolloth, South Africa

The nuggets in this book are catalysts to get back to the simple truth—love your God with all your heart, mind, and soul! Getting back the basics requires loads of unlearning. This book helps do that!

JAYANTH JESUDASAN
Chennai, India

Don Nori continues to encourage us to be a people who are after nothing less than knowing and manifesting the heart of God. Walking in the dreams of His heart.

MEGAN HAYES
Greensboro, NC

It's clear that as God reveals Himself to Don, he is filled with amazement and must share with others. No doubt *The God Watchers* will draw you in to a lifestyle of becoming a God Watcher, looking for God in any situation, at any given time.

JANET DOUGLAS
Evansville, Indiana

The God Watchers is wonderfully insightful. It offers an ingenious way of looking at your life and living for God. The clarity that comes from reading this book is great.

KADEN HURLEY
Newville, Pennsylvania

Don Nori, Sr. is one of my favorite authors because the Holy Ghost is his ghostwriter!

JEANIECE PEPPERS
Hoschton, Georgia

Don is a picture to me of the promise of God found in the Book of Jeremiah: *"You will seek Me and find Me, when you search for Me with all of your heart"* (Jer. 29:13). There is such an anointing on his writing it brings tears to my eyes and touches my heart—it makes me hungry for more!

KATHLEEN DESVOIGNE
Wilmington, North Carolina

We are the God Watchers. Thank you, Don Nori, Sr., for modeling this for us all. You are a voice that speaks from within the ranks of those who have entered into these truths and a hand that reaches down to lift those who are learning and maturing up into the ranks of the God Watchers.

STEPHEN HOLMSTOCK
Anchorage, Alaska

I am barely able to digest these awesome truths.

CLITA DIAS
Dubai, UAE

Thank you, Don, for expressing what I could not from within my own heart. It has given me great peace and comfort. Your humility and brokenness before the Lord makes you an approachable man of God, whose words are like the tip of a spear, piercing the soul and bringing healing.

AMY FRIEND
Divine Connection Ministries
Wilmington, Ohio

When we receive this understanding with our minds and hearts, the release is like dropping heavy baggage at a crosswalk and never turning back to pick it up. We were created to be filled with the life of Jesus, not the burdens of life. All of the answers to life's problems are found as we practice His presence.

LAURIE CHATFIELD
Raleigh, North Carolina

Don, you may be a passing vapor but your books and the message you bring will remain as a sweet-smelling fragrance to the Lord.

KIMBERLY EARL OGDEN
El Cajon, California

THE GOD WATCHERS

DESTINY IMAGE BOOKS BY DON NORI, SR.

DESTINY IMAGE MEDIA PRODUCTS BY DON NORI, SR.

THE GOD WATCHERS

JESUS DID WHAT HE SAW
HIS FATHER IN HEAVEN DOING

DON NORI SR.

DESTINY IMAGE₀ PUBLISHERS, INC.

P.O. Box 310, Shippensburg, PA 17257-0310

"Promoting Inspired Lives."

This book and all other Destiny Image, Revival Press, MercyPlace, Fresh Bread, Destiny Image Fiction, and Treasure House books are available at Christian bookstores and distributors worldwide.

For a U.S. bookstore nearest you, call 1-800-722-6774.

For more information on foreign distributors, call 717-532-3040.

Reach us on the Internet: www.destinyimage.com.

ISBN 13 TP: 978-0-7684-4245-8

ISBN 13 Ebook: 978-0-7684-8460-1

For Worldwide Distribution, Printed in the U.S.A.

1 2 3 4 5 6 7 8 / 18 17 16 15 14

CONTENTS

PREFACE

WHEN I FIRST FELT THE NUDGING OF THE HOLY SPIRIT TO write this book, I did not realize the scope of the work or the prophetic feeling that would overshadow me as I wrote. But that is normal when I start out on a project. The more I write, the more I hear, feel, sense, see. I am continuously struck with how the Lord is always speaking. That revelatory River of His presence within is always flowing, always refreshing, always renewing, teaching, healing, encouraging. Our Lord has much to say to humanity. He made us with the ability to live in communicational harmony with Him. Learning to stay continuously aware of that has become my life's obsession as I want more than anything for the world to see Him through me with as accurate a representation of Him as possible. To that end, I must decrease. He must increase. I must quiet my soul so I can hear Him.

These lessons are enriched in my heart every time I write. Every moment at the computer is an adventure, an anticipation of what will come next. This not to say, in any way whatsoever, that what I write is infallible. Yikes, that would be a scary thought. My goal is to hear as clearly as possible with the fleshly interference of my soul. You will be the judge of how well I have succeeded at that by discernment to separate flesh from Spirit.

I also have discovered that our Lord is speaking, flowing whether I am writing or not. I have learned that I can be conscious of this connection all the time. So can everyone who is willing to quiet themselves to see what He is doing. It is amazing, exciting, fulfilling, and it is for everyone. So if this book helps no one else, it has helped me immeasurably. It has opened me to greater reality of Him in the now as well as the certainty that as I live in the I AM, that awareness grows ever stronger.

You are actually watching the journey of my life. My books are like the roadway I am traveling in discovering the wonders of His mighty love. While I have to admit that roadway has more twists and turns than I had expected, it is also certain that it is my own humanity that makes the road as difficult as it appears. Jesus said, "My load is easy and my burden is light" (see Matt. 11:30). When that burden is more than I can bear, there is a reason for it. It is never His fault and rarely the enemy's fault. It is usually my own desperate humanity trying to get its own way. The enemy does not have the unfettered access we seem to believe he has. His power, access, and authority are limited to non-existent. I am hidden in Christ. That is either true or it is not.

So as you read these pages, you will be learning as I was being taught. I studied the Scriptures, being careful that the written word and Living Word were in harmony as I heard, saw, and wrote. If these pages help you, pass them on to another; better yet, let them buy their own copy!

God bless you with wisdom for the day, courage to see what you have never seen, and His manifest presence to be the Light for your path. But then, I believe you will. After all, I can sense your heart; you are just like me.

INTRODUCTION

WE LIVE ON THE CUSP OF THE MOST UNIMAGINABLE HAP-penings in the history of the human race. The lines that separate the natural and the spiritual are blurring in ways none could have ever foreseen. The hunger for the undiscov-ered is igniting a sense of daring into the hearts of believers all over the world. The Divine draw is giving many people the courage to look at things in ways that have been taboo for many generations. The reality of true encounters with God and carrying His nature, passion, and power to a world that is desperate for change is beginning to lead humankind, or whoever is willing, to the edge of accepted ideology and theology. I call it the undiscovered frontier or the brink of human disaster.

It is, of course, the realm of the Spirit where the intellec-tual cannot understand, the scientist cannot quantify, and the religious cannot imitate. In short, to those who will risk all, you, as a believer, will once again take the lead in exploring the things that most never knew were there to explore. This includes every strata of culture from science to art. But it also includes dimensions and spiritual reality we have yet to discover.

The wanderlust for meaning into Jesus's provocative words is sending average believers on adventures of discovery that will change the way we look at just about everything. Jesus seemed to drop tidbits of information to make us search for what the natural realm can only imagine and what the religious calls unlawful. Yet, for those who will not be satisfied with less, the fullness of His salvation manifest in time and space, there is no deterring them.

"SIR, WE WISH TO SEE JESUS."

Nature is in the throes of birth pangs. The Spirit of God is brooding, hovering, churning, wooing those who will see Him. There is a cry from the throne room of the Almighty. There is true eternal travail in the house where God lives—you and me.

He is gathering His people to Himself, for Himself, to do His bidding. Those who have quieted their soul already sense His passion and are responding to Him.

This is not a time for begging Him, advising Him, assuming His plan, His likes or dislikes. It is not a time to reinforce our personal doctrines or build our fleshly kingdoms. It is a time for seeing Him; for discerning His Presence and agreeing with what He wants to do on the earth. It is a time for Him to change our thoughts to His thoughts, our will to His will. Although most of us cannot fathom the possibility that we have any beliefs, doctrines, or building programs that are not His, I challenge you to do what I do: Give Him the opportunity to burn away everything that is not of Him. Lay everything on the altar of sacrifice and stand back. Whatever withstands the fire from heaven, take it back up again—it is yours or He would have burned it up.

The living Presence is about to give new credence to all we have thought we understood and believed. He is about to stand over our shoulders, as it were, to bring crisp understanding and true vision to the written Word, so that the Living Word might be more clearly imparted, experienced, and seen for who He really is. As the blinders are loosened, the veil taken away, let us be very careful not to be found trying to keep them in place. The fear of seeing the new things He wants us to do can be daunting, but we need to recognize that when we fear these things, it is usually evidence that we are truly seeing Him. This, again, is another reason that the spirit of discernment is vital. The fear of God can warn us and the fear of the unknown facets of God can draw us close to Him. We need to know the difference.

That means that the blinders must fall, even if it means being knocked off our spiritual horse as Saul was when he was determined to persecute the church Jesus was beginning to build. Saul's horse, his personal "high place," was his strength, his power, and a symbol of his authority. Make no mistake, there is no high place on earth that is too high for the Lord to reach. There is no "untouchable" person, no "safe haven" for the things that must come down. I say this with fear and trembling, for I am not immune to this any more than any others are. I have experienced this firsthand—it is humbling, indeed.

Deep calls to deep at the sound of Your waterfalls;
all Your breakers and Your waves have rolled over
me (Psalms 42:7).

When deep calls to deep, those who see the depths need to respond. He calls to all humanity with the same intensity, but not all of us are quieting ourselves to see Him or hear the groan from the reach of His heart. He does not respect one over another. In returning to the place of quietly watching Him, we are individually transformed, becoming salt to those who would be thirsty.

The most sacred prayer is simply, *"Thy kingdom come, Thy will be done, on earth and in me."* The single-minded, acutely focused heart has only one desire. That desire is to see Him above the fray of human emotion, human institutions, governments, old ideas, and weathered programs that have never stood the test of time, faith, or most importantly, the evidence of God in them. The single-minded heart passionately wants to see everything that stands in the way of seeing the Lord removed so that He, our Lord Jesus, might be clearly seen, understood, and trusted.

To that end, we must understand *The God Watchers* is God's plan, not man's. Jesus saw what His Father was doing and did the same thing. He saw the will of God and allowed His Father's will to flow from Him to the hungry, desperate masses of humanity.

God is drawing us from Holy Place experience to the Most Holy Place experience. We are crossing the River Jordan, as it were, moving from the wilderness to the Promised Land. For the children of Israel, everything changed once they crossed that river. Life was brand new. There was no more manna from heaven, no more falling meat, no more rock following them. They had to discover the wonders of the new land they were occupying, as well as the new threats as enemies abounded in this Promised Land. Those who can hear the Holy Spirit and see their Lord, pay attention! Everything is changing.

It is clear that the same transitions are happening now. Many love to proclaim this prophetic word today, but nearly no one is willing to embrace the new lifestyle that this new place in God demands. The old is passing away, behold everything is becoming new, from our vocabulary to our resting place; from our faith to our prayers; from Holy Spirit baptism to understanding the working of the Holy Spirit. The church, as most have known it, is changing. It is changing into something that is coming down from heaven through the likes of simple folk, average folks, hungry folks who understand that they have nothing to lose and everything to gain.

God watchers! Look up, our redemption comes!

Chapter 1

THE AWAKENING OF
A GOD WATCHER

I NEVER HAD A HERO. THERE WAS NEVER ANYONE I REALLY wanted to emulate. Sure, I loved my dad, but it never crossed my mind to be like him. He was a hard-working, loving family man. He spent tons of time with us, especially my twin brother Ron and I. We played football and baseball with him; went to the lake for swimming and picnics; even went to Pittsburgh Pirate baseball games. Yes, I loved him, but for some reason I did not imagine following in his footsteps.

As I grew up, I was never enticed to elevate anyone to the level of hero. Sure, I had a throb in my heart that I did not understand until many years later. I went to Mass, communion, and special services more often than most. I loved Jesus, but it never dawned on me that I might actually be able to experience His reality, His love, as deeply as I had loved Him. So I just chugged along with this yearning I did not know what to do with.

Then one night in 1968, I was watching the CBS Evening News with Walter Cronkite. He did a story that further fanned the flames of my heart. It was a story about an unusual phenomenon sweeping the United States among the youth. These young folks were doing most unusual things whilst so many others in their generation were discovering drugs and were part of the free sex "love" movement. The teens Walter Cronkite was talking about on this night were discovering God. They were also part of a "love" movement. But this was different. It had nothing to do with sex or drugs, but everything to do with God and one another. While I watched this short report, my heart yearned for that experience! "That is what I want," I cried to myself for days following, but I never thought in my wildest imagination that it would be possible for me. After all, really cool stuff only ever happened to other people.

As if God had heard the cry of my heart, our Catholic church arranged a youth retreat shortly after that. That sort of thing was very unusual back in those days, as teens were expected to get the message from the Mass like everyone else. It seemed there was a greater interest in learning the rules and getting the indoctrination at Mass than anything else. But in retrospect, I cannot help but think that this very unusual retreat was God-ordained. I immediately volunteered to help any way possible. I was there from morning till night. I was doing all sorts of things for the priest in charge of the event. It was a glorious time. I felt so fulfilled, so complete. I hated the thought of this time coming to an end. But it did. The retreat was over and so was my brief sense of fulfillment. But it made me even more dissatisfied than ever. I thought to myself again and again that there had to be more to this devotion to God than I was seeing or anyone was telling me.

But what could it possibly be? I was a good Catholic. I was an altar boy. I attended all the services during Lent. I fasted, prayed the rosary, built an altar to Mary every spring, went to confession often. I tried, tried, and tried again to be the kind of person who would please God. But somehow, it seemed that it was not possible to actually be forever satisfied. According to what I was taught, the sacraments were my best chance of getting close to God. Any other method was just plain wrong in the eyes of the church, therefore, quite impossible. I resigned myself to live without being able to touch the invisible, to talk to God, to know Him as I wanted to. He was far away. I loved Him so much it hurt, but He did not seem to return that love or even care for that matter.

But strange things seemed to happen to me. I remember as a ten-year-old kid absent-mindedly raising my hands during a worship song in the middle of the Mass. My father gently but quickly took my hands and lowered them. He looked around to see if anyone had seen it, then he looked at me with disapproving inquisitiveness. Heck, I didn't even understand what I did! I was glad that Dad never mentioned it to me. I would have had no answer for him!

One time my dad was sick with a severe back injury. He rolled back and forth in bed trying to find a way to sleep without pain. I watched him through the door that was cracked open. I could not stand to see him in pain, so I went to my room and fell on my bed. I don't know what I was thinking, but I prayed without a rosary, without a formulated, approved prayer, and without the sign of the cross. What was

I thinking? I didn't care. My dad was so very sick. I just wanted him to be better. I cried out to God that afternoon and experienced a miracle that no one has ever talked about. Most of my family does not, to this day, know about it. But when I was done praying, I returned to his room. Through the cracked door I could see him sitting up in bed and telling Mom the pain was gone…and it stayed gone! I burst into the room to tell them I was just praying for him and God healed my dad! Ha! No one shared my obvious enthusiasm, but I didn't care. From that moment on, I knew there was a way to reach my Lord, who was the secret love of my life.

Life goes on. It settled back down into the humdrum routine that was far from what I stubbornly knew was possible. My disillusionment only grew worse as I went away to college in Shippensburg, Pennsylvania. My frustration turned to anger and my anger turned to things I am not proud of, things better left unsaid and definitely left in the past. I will only say that I became known as the "hippie's hippie," or in more telling terms, the "freak's freak." I could have been the poster child for the local hippie/rebellion movement of the times.

Then came the proverbial straw that broke the camel's back. The conviction of the Lord over my many sins, coupled with an almost uncontrollable desire for my Lord brought me to a dramatic turning point. I would go to the priest. I would tell him everything. I would spill my guts to him, expose myself, let him see what was really in me and then I would wait and hope for the best.

After mustering up the nerve to go to confession at the local Catholic church, I walked into the confessional with hope and a great deal of fear in my heart. Instead of the kind, understanding, fatherly man I was hoping for, I was met with a very liberal priest who told me that all the things I was doing were just a part of exploring my new freedoms away from home as well as discovering my manhood. Therefore, they were not sins. He said everyone does things that they will later regret, but they were certainly nothing to worry about. "The good news for you is that you have not sinned. You and God are OK." I was devastated. I had been well aware of my manhood for years and I certainly did not need to discover anything more than I had already discovered. I left that confessional and the church more frightened than ever. Not only did I know for certain that I was doing wrong, but now I did not have a way back to God.

In the midst of this emotional turmoil, an unlikely messenger of the Lord came in the form of a less than respectable rock opera called *Jesus Christ Superstar*. Who would have ever thought that an opera touted as offensive and downright sacrilegious would be an important catalyst in bringing me the transforming encounter that changed my life forever? "Always hoped that I'd be an apostle," were the words of a song that caused my heart to burn with desire for the reality of God. At that time, I assumed that an apostle was the closest one could get to God and therefore that is what I wanted to be. I didn't know how to become one, but I wanted it with all my heart.

I did not understand what was happening to me during those days of rebirth but I was certain that something was out of my control deep in my heart. Something had to give. Something had to happen to get a handle on this raging fire of desperate desire in my heart. I played that opera a hundred times. I listened to it continuously day and night for weeks. It was the only thing in the entire world that spoke what I was feeling, what I wanted, what I needed. Nothing else mattered in my life, not classes, not friends, not family, not church. I was becoming single-minded; my focus was clear and my determination absolute. I was becoming a God watcher.

It would not be long until I finally came face to face with the Lover of my soul. An unlikely event brought me to an unlikely young lady whom God would use to change my life forever. But it would be weeks before I could even begin to verbalize what had happened to me. It felt as though I were a butterfly emerging from a cocoon. Everything was new, brand new. I had begun a new life, a new series of adventures that would redirect my life's aimlessness and put it on course to things I could not imagine and even today find so hard to believe.

This young lady, as it turns out, is now my wife Cathy. We have been on this adventure together for over forty years and it just really does get more exciting together. But our first few meetings were all business, so to speak. Already a believer, she was eager to share her story of how God saved her from a life of fear, loneliness, drugs, etc. She had all my attention, for more than one reason I might add. Cathy introduced me to other really old people like Pastor Ted and Lou Yohe, Jean Warren, and others who were in their early thirties. As an avowed rebel, it was hard to listen to them at first, but their words, the fire in their eyes, the peace in their smiles just fanned the fire within my heart. Two weeks later, Cathy told me I should picture a door in front of my heart. "Just picture

Jesus knocking on that door. Invite Him in. Tell Him you are sorry for your sins, that you want to live for Him. He will come in and certainly change your life." Cathy's words were more than I could bear. That night I experienced Jesus for the first time with an ecstatic realization that He loved me as much as I loved Him!

I found many answers from those who wonderfully guided me through those early years. They laid a foundation in my life that has kept me true to Him. Nonetheless, that inner fire, inner gnawing, although satisfied in part, continued to rage and kept me searching for a deeper reality than I had experienced. Though I have found much in Him to satisfy my soul, that eternal fire within me rages still, often quite uncontrollably. There was a time when I wondered why this hunger never seemed to be satisfied, but I soon realized that it was that hunger that kept me focused on Him. Hunger was not a bad thing. Thirst was not a bad thing. Just as it is in our natural bodies, these feelings of hunger and thirst keep us pursuing Him for the satisfaction of our souls.

It took years for me to discover the secrets that I am sharing in this book. I am probably a little dense, for I am certain He was trying to show me, long before I was able to see, how easy it really is to see what He is doing.

At the end of the day, I have discovered that satisfaction and fulfillment only come from doing what He is doing, saying what He is saying, being who He is in me. When co-laboring with Him, being in sync with His desires brings a peace that cannot be explained or shaken. I am truly on the cutting edge of His plan for me. It truly is the peace that passes all understanding.

This was the very beginning of a journey toward being the kind of God watcher who not only watches God, but responds to Him.

Chapter 2

ENCOUNTERING JESUS, THE CONSUMMATE GOD WATCHER

He who has My commandments and keeps them is the one who loves Me; and he who loves Me will be loved by My Father, and I will love him and will disclose Myself to him (JOHN 14:21).

IN 1988, I HAD A SUCCESSFUL MINISTRY IN MANY, MANY ways. Although Destiny Image was in its infancy and we struggled daily to keep the doors open, we kept on. I had a very active preaching ministry. I prayed for the sick, dealt very successfully with demonic activity, and was getting more invitations than I knew what to do with. But I knew something was not right. I was still not satisfied. I was not fulfilled. I remember telling the Lord that there had to be more than I was experiencing. I felt like such a heretic. I was redeemed, filled with the Holy Spirit, functioning in all the gifts of the Spirit, and like the rich young ruler I was asking the Lord, "What do I still lack?" There was silence from heaven, which in itself was my answer. I had to look for it.

The next few years were frustrating, lonely, and frightening. I began seeing life within the veil of Most Holy Place, the realm of Spirit that I had come to call "all God." I began to see union with God, the virgin church that Jesus is building, and the glorious Kingdom of God on earth. I began sharing what I was seeing. I had always preached my journey, so it was natural to talk about what I was finding. Well, it was not very popular, to say the least. Back in those days, these topics were even scarier to talk about than they are now! A well-meaning friend with an important international ministry took me aside to "show me the way more accurately." He advised that these topics were diversions from Truth. I was going to mess myself up and wreck the possibility of future ministry. In effect, I had to get with the program. But his gentle and loving rebuke only fired my heart. I wanted Him. "Those who hunger and thirst for righteousness will be satisfied," Jesus said (see Matt. 5:6). I wasn't satisfied. Needless to say, I did not get with the program. Instead, I searched more passionately.

Eventually, the walk became more and more lonely. I wondered if I had indeed gone off the deep edge of heresy with these glorious things I was seeing. I wondered why I did not hear things from others. Why was I the only one seeing them? Of course, God is faithful. In time I found that I was certainly not the only one talking about these things. God was speaking and many were hearing the same things I was hearing and seeing in Him. God watchers seldom have the comfort of others in the early days. But be assured, you are definitely not alone!

But at that time, I was alone and my heart ached and ached for Him. Though I had little support, I kept searching. I must admit that I was close to giving up completely. But just in the nick of time, I began to experience Him and His manifest Presence. Soon, what I was preaching in theory had indeed become reality in a small way in my life. As time went on, being encouraged by these exciting but rare times of close encounter, the Word began to open up to me in new and experiential ways. I am not able to put a time to when I realized that much of what I had believed was just dead wrong, but a new awakening gradually began in my heart that continues unabated to this day. I was discovering that there *is* much to be discovered, that He *does* want a personal relationship with His people. In fact, Jesus suffered and died so He could have an interactive and personal relationship with all humanity. I discovered that the brink of heresy was far different from heresy; there was more to Him than I was ever told. It was at this point that I put everything I had ever been told on the altar of sacrifice. "Burn away what was never from You, my Lord, and strengthen what is from Your heart." That is the prayer that kept me hopeful and to this day keeps my life with Him a life of powerful discovery, adventure, and love.

My Search into Holy Simplicity

The secret was so simple I missed it for years. Just like the man who could not see the forest because there were too many trees, I could not see Him for the myriad of things that are supposedly required of all believers in Jesus. While others were telling me to follow them, listen to them, and do what they asked, the yearning of my spirit would not settle for it. There was more—a lot more. I wanted to see Him, to experience Him face to Face.

Then one day the words of Jesus jumped off the page and into my heart as I was reading.

> *Therefore Jesus answered and was saying to them, "Truly, truly, I say to you, the Son can do nothing of Himself, unless it is something He sees the Father doing; for whatever the Father does, these things the Son also does in like manner"* (John 5:19).

Could it be that simple? Could it be that we have made following the Lord much harder than it needed to be? Could it be that this life in Christ is not impossible? Jesus watched His Father. Whatever Jesus saw His Father doing *there*, in the heavens, He did it *here on the earth*. In fact, Jesus was so surrendered to His Father, that His Father could do His work through the yielded life of Jesus. Our Father wants the same for us.

As I continued my studies I found a more correct rendering of the verse, one that adheres more closely to the Greek grammar usage. This more accurate Greek translation of John 5:19 is presented by Dr. Thomas Gardner:

> *"It is impossible for the Son to do anything unless He sees the Father doing it."*

This statement absolutely reflected the passion of my heart's desire. I wanted to be so one with Him that I literally could not do anything unless He did it through me.

My heart leaped for joy, the embers smoldering in my soul jumped once again into a raging fire at the possibility of such union with God. I held my heart lest what I thought might somehow not be true. I began a search of the words of Jesus. I had spent my life listening to others teach me about His words and what He expected. This time, I would search Him out myself, carefully studying and carefully listening for what He had to say about Himself and how He related to His Father in heaven.

ALWAYS PLEASING TO THE FATHER

And He who sent Me is with Me; He has not left Me alone, for I always do the things that are pleasing to Him (John 8:29).

"I want to do what pleases Him!" I shouted out loud. "Nothing satisfies me more than knowing I am doing what my Lord wants me to do."

In a moment of time, I began to sense spiritual rest in knowing that I could, and in many ways I was, indeed, doing God's will. Sure, it didn't happen overnight. I had a lot of old programming to clear out of my mind. A lot of wood, hay, and stubble had to burn away. I have lots of old memories, pain, and disappointment to sift through. But with His leading, that is happening. I am growing into this place day by day. I've learned that the accomplishments of today will not satisfy me tomorrow. I want to be even more in sync with

Him tomorrow than I am today. A new life is emerging, a new life 60 years in the making. But a new life nonetheless.

MY FOOD

> Jesus said to them, "My food is to do the will of Him who sent Me and to accomplish His work" (John 4:34).

Ha! No kidding! I can go to a hundred meetings, read a dozen books, listen to worship music 24/7, and still feel unfulfilled, hungry. But *doing* the will of God really does satisfy the longing of my soul.

Knowing that I am doing His word and not just hearing it gives me the confidence that I am truly in relationship with the One I truly, unashamedly love and adore. As I began to test this new thought, allowing it to digest in my spirit, my life began to change once again. I had discovered a secret that really wasn't a secret at all, for it was all there on nearly every page of the Holy Scriptures. Jesus wants *followers!*

Here are just three examples

> Now as Jesus was walking by the Sea of Galilee, He saw two brothers, Simon who was called Peter, and Andrew his brother, casting a net into the sea; for they were fishermen. And He said to them, "Follow Me, and I will make you fishers of men." Immediately they left their nets and followed Him (Matthew 4:18-20).

> Going on from there He saw two other brothers, James the son of Zebedee, and John his brother, in

the boat with Zebedee their father, mending their nets; and He called them. Immediately they left the boat and their father, and followed Him (Matthew 4:21-22).

As Jesus went on from there, He saw a man called Matthew, sitting in the tax collector's booth; and He said to him, "Follow Me!" And he got up and followed Him (Matthew 9:9).

Followers *follow*. Very deep, isn't it? Followers look at what their Master is doing and they do the same thing. The key is to watch what He is doing and do it too. I began to see that it was far more than just watching to imitate what the Master is doing. The goal is to become like Him. Becoming like Him would be a whole new issue.

A pupil is not above his teacher; but everyone, after he has been fully trained, will be like his teacher (Luke 6:40).

Becoming like Him would require a lot of time with Brokenness so that I could easily yield my way, my desires, even my prized religious doctrines to Him, that He might freely live His glorious life through me. This is truly the only food that satisfies the soul.

I've learned that satisfaction does not come from attending more meetings or more Bible studies; it comes from doing the will of God. There is no doubt that God will place you among believers who will give you the solid foundation in Christ. The key is to be among those who truly have your best interests at heart and who also have an actual interactive relationship with Jesus. It was such an amazing revelation to me. At that time I was attending every meeting, Bible study, and work day at the church. I gave till it hurt, but none of it satisfied me. Then I began seeing Him and nothing has been the same since.

JESUS, THE MASTER OF SIMPLICITY

> *For I did not speak on My own initiative, but the Father Himself who sent Me has given Me a commandment as to what to say and what to speak. I know that His commandment is eternal life; therefore the things I speak, I speak just as the Father has told Me* (John 12:49-50).

Just how did Jesus do it? He lived in a time of no technological advantage. He was an obscure man from an obscure little town in a near useless desert country as part of an empire that considered Israel little more than a pebble stuck under the king's sandal. Without money, advisors, marketing, or a preaching schedule, in just three years He established a global movement that continues to this day, having profoundly affected world history for over 2,000 years. How did He do it? The answer is simple. He was a God watcher. All He basically did was see what His Father was doing and He did it too.

Think about it. By doing only what He saw the Father doing, Jesus's ministry was just as limited as it was expansive. For instance, He only healed one person among hundreds at the pool of Bethesda, though He could have healed them all, and many other times did exactly that. Why? Because He was watching what His Father was doing and only did what He saw. In the same way, He chose only twelve specific men to be His apostles, though He could have chosen a multitude. He did not feed everyone He spoke to, although hunger was a pressing concern. He started no schools, never took an offering, never set an advanced schedule of meetings. This list of things He did not do is endless. But what He did do is certain. He saw what His Father in heaven was doing and did the same thing.

> *I can do nothing on My own initiative. As I hear,*
> *I judge; and My judgment is just, because I do not*
> *seek My own will, but the will of Him who sent Me*
> (John 5:30).

When Jesus did something He saw His Father doing, miracles happened. He never had to resort to coaxing, prodding, guilt, or tricks to bring forth the Father's will to earth. He simply stepped into what He saw in the Spirit and participated in God's active will for that moment. The things of the Spirit realm poured into our dimension through the obedience of Jesus, who did only what He saw the Father pouring into our dimension. I am reminded of His prayer:

> *Your kingdom come. Your will be done, on earth*
> [this dimension] *as it is in heaven* [dimension of
> His origin] (Matthew 6:10).

Jesus spoke of this incredible continuous experience of being a conduit through which heaven transforms earth when He said:

Whatever you bind on earth shall have been bound in heaven; and whatever you loose on earth shall have been loosed in heaven (Matthew 18:18).

The ministry of Jesus was so simple that it is difficult to accept. We are always trying to come up with a religious formula for success, for bringing the Kingdom into earth. But as we watch Jesus it becomes apparent that true ministry is really just that simple: we are to simply see what our Father is doing in heaven and allow Him to do the same through us. Our challenge is our willingness to silence our souls so we can actually participate in God-breathed activity.

There is so much more to be seen and experienced. God wants to show the precious things of His heart to us. These things are waiting in Spirit for us to see them.

Chapter 3

GOD WATCHERS SEE BEYOND

*Beloved, now we are children of God,
and it has not appeared as yet what we
will be. We know that when He appears,
we will be like Him, because we will
see Him just as He is* (1 JOHN 3:2).

WHAT SATISFIES THE SOUL OF MAN?

HAVE YOU DISCOVERED THAT THIRST IS NOT QUENCHED AND hunger is not satisfied by the miraculous? Miracles are like eating ice cream—it tastes good, feels good, but does not nourish the body. In fact, ice cream only makes us fat. Miracles are the same. They simply point to the One who does the miracles, but in themselves they cannot satisfy the inner craving of our hearts. We are satisfied by His presence, His Spirit

39

reassuring our spirits that we are His and He is ours. Yes, true relationship, union with Him happens through a miracle that the five senses cannot begin to touch. The reality of His manifest presence cannot compare with the "ice cream" of a miracle. But do not misunderstand me. I love miracles! I love to see my Lord showing Himself powerful to the world. My reference is toward those seasoned believers who try to get inner fulfillment by miracles, manifestations, and angels. Outward evidence is powerful, exciting, and encouraging, but it is just ice cream compared to the succulent steak His presence offers believers at any age.

It is true that when we see Him as He is, we become like Him. The more we see Him, the more His passion begins to rule our heart. His love begins to flood our soul. We begin to respond to the Holy Spirit as Jesus responded when He walked the earth. There is little significance in me as a mere man, but there is full assurance, full completion of His love in Him. We often believe we can go it in our strength from Him. It is as though we believe the natural gifts God gives us are almost enough to fulfill our destiny. But the personal talents and gifts God gives us blossom exponentially when we yield everything we have and everything we are to Jesus. For we who believe are more than mere humans. We are human vessels filled with God. So we are becoming all God-filled believers just as Jesus was.

For it was the Father's good pleasure for all the fullness to dwell in Him (Colossians 1:19).

There is no doubt that absolutely everything changes when we see this, for as we see Him as He truly is, the miraculous process of brokenness begins, changing us into ones who display Him in broken humility. The world starves for those who have truly seen Him, for from the believer's own brokenness he feeds not just himself, but the world as well. We do not understand the power of adversity. We usually try to pray our way out of adversity without even thinking that we could be experiencing a problem specifically so we can learn something. When we just focus on getting out without learning something, we really do waste our sorrows.

WHAT EXACTLY IS A GOD WATCHER?

A God watcher is one who sees, perceives, senses, feels, and hears what is on God's heart. He can put the activity, plan, or intention of God into clearly understood words. The God watcher can discern a particular circumstance; he can know the wind of the Holy Spirit through time; he can convey the emotion of our Lord and see the wisdom of God for a person, city, or nation. A God watcher "sees" what God is doing and, opening his heart, he allows the Lord Jesus do the same thing through him. All of us can be, or shall I say *should be*, God watchers. The ministry of a prophet as well as the gift of prophecy should not be confused with being a God watcher. The prophetic ministries in the church Jesus is building have more specialized tasks for the church and the world at large. But as for watching God, that is the personal responsibility as well as the privilege for all those who call Him Lord.

ANYONE CAN BE A GOD WATCHER

In fact, God has made every one of us with the ability to see Him. It is part of His overall intention for us as a race.

We are made with the tools we need to see Him. Unfortunately, not everyone has given themselves to experience Him in all His fullness. But make no mistake. He wants you to see Him, understand Him, and communicate His plan and presence to all the world. No matter what your interest may be, God is already doing it. If you watch what He does, you will have the confidence to yield to Him so He can do it His way through you.

How Does the God Watcher See?

"Seeing" God is a bit of a misnomer. The Scriptures use the word *see* for lack of a better word in our language. To "see" in the Spirit is to observe God in the dimension of eternity. It is the other-worldly ability to be in tangible, cognitive, and interactive contact with the Spirit of God. Any believer can be a conduit of His presence between this dimension and eternity. A God watcher has allowed himself to be taught of the Lord in the ability to discern and interpret the activity of the Spirit. Any of our senses can "see" what He is doing. The goal is to have this interactive, cognitive, and continuous relationship with Him whereby we can accurately see, perceive, and allow Him to do His work through us. It is not that we are doing what He is doing. Rather, when we see Him, we are more likely to allow Him to work through us, no matter how "out of the ordinary" it appears to be. We will subconsciously resist anything that comes to mind that is beyond what we can accept in our lives. Of course, that is why so many of us are stuck where we are.

It will take determination and practice to allow Jesus to work His mighty works through us. For one thing, we usually see His mighty works as moving mountains, raising the dead, etc. But His mighty works also include giving ourselves to love, serve, and honor those whom God causes to cross my path.

In the past, I found myself looking at everyone as a potential person for me to display God's power on. (Let the reader take note.) But I have discovered that God causes folks to cross my path for one reason only—to love them. I no longer anticipate what that might mean. I am simply myself. I am no longer trying to figure out what Jesus would do. I yield so He can love them through me.

These, then, are just the beginnings of the mighty works of God through those who will yield. I cannot predict what comes next. I don't even try. *I am* as *He is*.

GOD WATCHERS ARE DISCIPLINED

Our world is filled with more than enough distractions to keep us focused on the things that will dissolve at the end. It is not that these things are unimportant. When our senses are distracted, consumed with temporal things, the things eternal are neglected—lost, as it were, from our focus.

The glitz and glitter of the fading glory will always be grabbing our attention. This is not to mention the glitz and glitter of the world. God watchers are focused on Him and are training themselves not to be so easily turned by the things that look good but are failing. Remember, Moses was filled with a fading glory; that is why he covered his head. He did not want the people seeing what was fading from his life. Glitz and glitter exist in this world and in the Spirit. If our eyes are focused continuously on Him and where He is leading us, we will not be so easily drawn to the things from yesterday, no matter how powerful they were back in the day.

> *Then I turned to see the voice that was speaking with me. And having turned I saw...* (Revelation 1:12).

Systems of religion, pious as they have been seen, are the fading glory of yesterday's manna. God is moving us on. We have an important choice today. Either we fade with the passing glory of what mesmerizes the carnal and religious or we move on to experience and become the unapproachable light of His presence as He shines through simple folks like you and me.

To be disciplined in our hearing, seeing, turning, and discerning is the goal of every God watcher. It is certainly my goal too. I have no greater passion than to be an accurate representation of His life and love to all those with whom I come into contact.

God Watchers Are Focused

God watchers are not just focused, they have a one-track mind. God has proven to these folks time and again that their own plans cannot stand the storm, will never be a shelter for the oppressed. They are coming to the simple revelation that God's plan is the only one that is the real tower of strength and hope.

So these folks watch God.

They want to see what He is doing. They do not second guess Him to try to convince Him of the validity of their plans. Brokenness has taught them that trusting in the Lord means that even when it looks as though His plan might not be as secure as they would like it to be, they move forward with what He is saying. Yes, it requires courage. Paul said he died daily. I am discovering why. You must walk away from, die to, your own ambitions, your fears, your pride for the immeasurable worth of knowing, seeing, turning, and perceiving Him.

Sure there are distractions—those shiny things that seem to glitter out of the corner of the eye, things that tempt us to sidestep the path He has put us on. But there will always be those things that tempt the ego, the selfishness, the lusts, the hurt, etc. Nonetheless, seeing Him outshines those distractions if we allow Him to fill our hearts with His dreams. I am motivated by this thought. I know He is dreaming dreams for my life. I may not know what they are, but I know they are there. With peace, rest, and gratitude, I move forward knowing each step I take is a step in God's will. The evidence of this? I am trusting Him. If I make a misstep, the next step is one that brings me back to where I should be. So each day is important. I am never waiting. I am always fulfilling. What I do right now has eternal significance. To not see this is to not understand the ways of eternity. He sees what we cannot. I walk in that knowledge.

CARRIERS OF ANOTHER SOUND

I am amazed when I think of all the time I spent trying to be like Him, look like Him, act like Him. When I am trying to merely act like Him, I am determining what *I* think He wants to do and then doing it in my own strength. I am like a radio trying to deliver sound to the hearer when there is no signal. Since there is no radio station for the radio to receive, the radio produces only static. But when a radio is tuned in to a station, the static of its own making gives way to the sound of the broadcast. The radio then is able to be what it was always intended to be—a connection between radio waves you cannot hear and the sounds the radio waves bring to your ear.

In the same way, when we are connected to Him instead of something else, we also become what we were always intended to be—a portal between this dimension and His, through which He flows, not by radio waves, but by the waves of the Holy Spirit. A radio is not intended to produce its own sound, which turns out to be static, noise unpleasant to the ear. It is intended to be a carrier of sound produced by another. So am I. I yield my spirit to Him, give my soul to Him and He literally lives His life through me.

When I see Him, I want to do what He is doing. As a result, I yield in eagerness, knowing He will work His own works through me. The advantage of seeing what He wants to do helps me agree with Him rather than resist His work, which is what we usually do in our own strength, our own intellect. Remember, we are His friends. He shows His friends what He is doing. Our Lord tells us His plan so we can flow with His plan. The unspiritual, the unyielded, the religious will never see Him. They only see what someone else has seen and hear only what their past experiences, good and bad, have said to them. Those who have given themselves to hear Him in the Spirit have determined to turn to Him at the sound of His Voice instead of continually responding to the things of our past, the things that keep us living in the five senses instead of living in the Spirit.

LEARNING TO INTERPRET THE THINGS OF THE SPIRIT

As the five senses put us in touch with this dimension of time and space, our spirit puts us in touch with the Spirit. Just as we need to be taught to interpret the signals our senses deliver to our brain, we also need to be taught how to interpret the signals that come to our brain from the Spirit.

The sensation "cold" is felt at any age but it is not defined as cold until we are able to be taught what that sensation is as well as remember it for the next time we feel cold. The brain has now learned that feeling and how to respond to it. So it is with the Spirit realm. We need to learn what the spiritual sensations we get mean; then we know how to respond to them.

The signals, sensations, and feelings that are transmitted to our brains teach us about that dimension. As we listen, we learn and become more mature. The realm of Spirit is new to us when we first experience it. Unlike maturing in the natural senses where there is plenty of help and instruction, the spiritual dimension is not that easily learned. There are few who can really teach what the feelings are and how to discern them. This has to be learned. It does not happen automatically.

We must make a conscious effort to silence our lives so we can hear from the Spirit. We do not take signals from more than one dimension at a time. At least, I don't—yet. I need to silence the natural input of the world so I can hear, perceive, understand, and discern what I am hearing in the Spirit. This is a process that takes time and practice. But soon a God watcher finds that he is always tuned to Him and is able to see what is controlling the circumstances of time and space without the hindrances of natural bias.

If we are determined to see God with the five senses and intellect alone (i.e., the soulish realm), we fall into error. Worse than that, though, we begin to be led by natural inclinations while we attribute those feelings to the spirit realm. To be sure, the demonic will certainly tickle our fleshly fancy in order to keep us from exercising our largely unused spiritual senses. These fleshly attractions will misdirect our discernment and delude us into thinking we are seeing the Lord when, in fact, we are only seeing a soulish reflection of our own deeply hidden human desires. The result is that we are doomed to a life of frustration, disappointment, and futile searches for His reality in a realm in which He cannot be seen.

> *God, give us discernment to discern flesh from spirit, to see the humanity and the spiritual separately! Give us the courage to confess and repent, if necessary, the fleshly desires we have so we can rightly watch what You are doing and then step into that instead of repeating the mistakes of the past.*

BE EQUALLY YOKED, SOUL TO THE SPIRIT

> *For I know that nothing good dwells in me, that is, in my flesh; for the willing is present in me, but the doing of the good is not* (Romans 7:18).

Remembering who we are without Him is our best way to filter out the advances of the enemy in our soul. To accept the bankrupt condition of our soul apart from union with the Spirit is to leave us with the alternative of seeking Him where He is, in Spirit and in truth. The vast opportunity we have in Him is left largely untapped as long as we think our hope is in our own earthy abilities. For sure, our God-given talents, once united with Him, can produce a life that is greater than we could ever imagine. No wonder Paul wants us to walk by the Spirit!

> *But I say, walk by the Spirit, and you will not carry out the desire of the flesh. For the flesh sets its desire against the Spirit, and the Spirit against the flesh; for these are in opposition to one another, so that you may not do the things that you please* (Galatians 5:16-17).

Many use this verse only in reference to sin, but the reference goes far deeper than that. The lusts of the flesh encompass the whole person's desire to do what he wants to do rather than respond to what he or she sees Him doing. Abandoning the lusts of the flesh also means leaving everything behind that is a hindrance. Of course, it means sin, but it also includes things we normally do not call sin but they are things that hold us back. Some of these include doctrine, hurts from the past, secret ambition, and poor self-image.

But just as the soul in union with the flesh skews our journey and will never allow us to reach our potential, union with the Spirit produces life, wholeness, courage, discernment, hope, and an endless array of powerful experiences found in the depth of God. The best motivation to be connecting our soul to our spirit is this promise of joy unspeakable and full of endless, fulfilling divine adventures.

GOD WATCHERS ARE NOT MADE IN A DAY

God watchers did not become that way overnight. It takes a lifetime of fine-tuning to become as sensitive to the Spirit as He wants us to be. But that does not mean we are ineffective until some day in the far-off future. Every day is today. Every moment we are present with our Father I AM is an experience of a lifetime.

But it is not natural for the five senses to perceive the spiritual realm. Our five senses detect data in this dimension. Our spirit detects the things that are undetectable to our earthy senses. The controlling forces of our natural realm function in a dimension of reality that requires a completely different set of senses to see. Those who understand this have an important edge over those who do not. So in reality, we have two sets of senses reporting to our soul. One set is solely responsible for seeing into the spirit while one set is responsible for our life in time and space.

To "see" Him is much more than meets the eye (pun intended). For to see Him is to understand that He lives in every dimension of reality, every dimension of emotion, thought, and action. To see Him is to realize that no matter how hard we try, we can never become what we are meant to be without Him. I have come to the conclusion after trying and trying—quite unsuccessfully, I might add—that there is only one way to really respond to what He is doing. That one way is to surrender. Yep, I quit trying. But it was then I saw that that was His desire all along. To see Him is to yield to Him. To yield to Him is to relinquish control of my life. When I relinquish control, I am asking Him to do what only He can do through me.

I am sure this is why I love God's rest. When I am resting in His love, His dreams for me, His strength and protection, I can go anywhere and do anything.

But there is a haunting verse that captures me and draws me to do whatever it takes to know Him now, in the fellowship of His suffering in order to experience the power of His resurrection. I hear the Lord Jesus calling me from deep within myself:

> *Who is this coming up from the wilderness, leaning on her beloved?* (Song of Solomon 8:5)

It is I, Lord! Not in my strength, my wit, or my ability, but leaning on You!

Chapter 4

JESUS IS BUILDING HIS HOUSE

For we are God's fellow workers; you are God's field, God's building. According to the grace of God which was given to me, like a wise master builder I laid a foundation, and another is building on it. But each man must be careful how he builds on it. For no man can lay a foundation other than the one which is laid, which is Jesus Christ. Now if any man builds on the foundation with gold, silver, precious stones, wood, hay, straw, each man's work will become evident; for the day will show it because it is to be revealed with fire, and the fire itself will test the quality of each man's work. If any man's work which he has built on it remains, he will receive a reward. If any man's work is burned up, he will suffer loss; but he himself will be saved, yet so as through fire (1 CORINTHIANS 3:9-15).

THIS SCRIPTURE IS A SOBER REMINDER THAT HE INTENDS TO build His own house, His own Kingdom, His own family. Building anything else and posturing that work as though it is of God is doomed to fail, as we said earlier. He knows exactly what He wants and exactly how He wants it to look. Although His church may vary from city to city, country to country, person to person, He shines from them the same anywhere in the world. It is amazing that even without knowing the language of a country I visit, the presence of God, the flow of His Holy Spirit is unmistakable.

Over the years, I have seen Him shine His light in barns, cathedrals, living rooms, tents, mobile homes, igloos, hotel conference rooms, classrooms, fire halls, schools, under the stars, and in churches. My, the list is endless. I see Him manifest His presence in meetings where the worship band is in the front of the people, behind the people, or in the midst of the people. I have experienced His presence in worship services where recorded music was used and where there was no music at all. The key in any place you want to experience Him is the condition of your heart. He will always respond to a heart of open desire, need, and desperation for Him.

So many seem to go on unaware that that there is Someone who is watching us. He really does want folks to carry out His plan in time and space. Jesus said that He only did what He saw His Father in heaven doing. I am certain that life would be far less random if I simply did what I saw Him doing. It is not that God's activity is random. It is that my seeing and responding to Him is random. Lord, help us to be consistent watchers! It is in the moment by moment response to what I see Him do now that will display His plan to the earth and lead me to destiny's next call.

If we really believed that God was watching us, was within us, has His own agenda, that it matters what we say and do—I wonder how that would change us? Would we really think we can do some of the things we do in the name of Jesus? Yikes. That'll make ya think!

Unfortunately, I personally struggle with only doing what everyone around me wants me to do, instead of doing what I see my Father doing. I wonder how many wood huts I have built over the years? How many straw shacks did I preside over? I am walking more circumspectly than I have ever walked before in my life. I have learned that it is far better to build nothing than to build with material that cannot withstand the storms that always come our way. These wood and hay cottages look so cute, but they will blow over at the slightest storm. Those who run to them for safety from the storm will be in big trouble.

I can almost see Jesus carefully looking over the plans of man to build their churches. He stops, turns to us, and says, "Hummm, I will build my own church and the gates of hell will not prevail against it." I bet He also adds, "You all can oversee this church, if you follow my instructions."

DISCERNING HIS WAYS FROM THE WAYS OF MAN

Within the world of the church system, the structures of man are easily recognized by the discerning. Their telltale signs include the glitter of the building and those "anointed" to build; the inordinate amount of time spent on raising money; the spiritually fleshly parlor tricks used to dupe the folks into greater giving; rewarding givers or those with special talents with special or prominent unearned positions in the structure of the organization. I wonder if these folks actually think they see Jesus doing these shady deals in the Spirit. I may not be an expert on how God does things, but I am fairly certain that He does not manipulate, intimidate, or make outrageous bargains just to get our time, money, and loyalty.

It requires the sweaty efforts of God-vacant struggles to build something that cannot pass the test of being God-breathed. Even though at first they might appear to work for a season, soon the stench of human initiative and fleshly programs will reveal themselves as the God-vacant kingdoms of those who have not allowed Brokenness to do her life-changing work deep within them. But here is the key: true God watchers have only His will as their goal. They are not anxious for recognition, titles, or authority. They simply are eternally tied to one passion—doing what they know their heavenly Father is doing.

Let this be fair warning—we do not start out as broken vessels, prepared for His use. Our beginnings are usually driven by the desire for recognition, approval, popularity, and need for authority. Brokenness has taught me over time that there is no replacement for the valley of the shadow of death. It is there, in the crucible of human life, that we lay down our will for His, our passion for His, and ultimately our life for His life. At some point in the valley, you will confess as John the Baptizer did, "He must increase and I must decrease." This is when you can be certain that you are in His will and turn the page on your growth in Him. For now the stench of fleshly desires begins to wane and the sweet fragrance of His presence arises from deep within your heart.

Never underestimate the accuracy of the feelings you get when something just doesn't seem to be right. We are taught not to judge another, but we can certainly understand the spirits are tested when someone filled with the Spirit and devoted to Jesus enters the room. It is not judgment to walk away from something you feel is not right. It is self-defense as well as self-preservation and God gives us those feelings specifically to warn us. Certainly, however, this is not a license to tell everyone what you are feeling, as any response needs to be done with prayer and humility. I speak of these things to demonstrate how discernment plays such a critical part in what we see, approve of, and participate in. Although this book may be a help to you, it will never replace time in His presence as the proper plumb line as to what is of God and what is not.

The common denominator is the Spirit of Jesus, Himself. He confirms to our heart what we see and hear in the Spirit, giving us the ability and the desire to separate soul from spirit. There are many so-called prophets who can read the air—that is, the aura, the shine of our spirit that emanates all around us. Reading the soul is akin to fortune-telling and not difficult to do. Most believers are so open that who they are hangs in the spirit like a banner around their neck. Whilst it is important to the love and ministry of others, that openness needs to be tempered with discernment. Just because I am thirsty I will not drink water from a stream that has an odor. The same is true with our spiritual thirst. Be careful what you drink. There is so much to this to discuss, but that is for another book.

SEEING AND HEARING OUR LORD JESUS

These issues may seem to be trivial, but they are the things that keep us from the intended goal of seeing Him, hearing the Father's Voice, and being a trumpet for that Voice among men. To be sure, there are many trumpets, many voices vying for our attention, our allegiance, and our obedience. But only His Voice will cause the Christ of God within to leap for joy. This, for lack of a better term, is the confirmation, the witness that we are indeed hearing His Voice. Consider these verses:

> Now at this time Mary arose and went in a hurry to the hill country, to a city of Judah, and entered the house of Zacharias and greeted Elizabeth. When Elizabeth heard Mary's greeting, the baby leaped in her womb; and Elizabeth was filled with the Holy Spirit. And she cried out with a loud voice and said, "Blessed are you among women, and blessed is the fruit of your womb! And how has it happened to me, that the mother of my Lord would come to me? For behold, when the sound of your greeting reached my ears, the baby leaped in my womb for joy. And blessed is she who believed that there would be a fulfillment of what had been spoken to her by the Lord" (Luke 1:39-45).

Jesus Christ, who lives within us, recognizes the Voice of God. The Voice cannot be faked. If the Voice is speaking, Christ within responds accordingly. Our response is usually similar to Elizabeth's response. As Christ leaps within us, we respond with something that confirms what we have heard. Elizabeth cried out, "Blessed are you among women." We respond when we hear His Voice as well, whether the Voice is directly to our heart, in a song, or a speaker. Some will respond with, "Amen!" or "Hallelujah!" Some will shout, "Praise God!" "That's right!" or a million other variations that are simply responses to the witness of the Voice. This inner witness is how we know we are hearing from the Lord. These kinds of responses throughout history were just not among Pentecostals, but were part of the normal expression of Christian life whether you are in the marketplace, the gathering place, or with other believers.

WHAT HAPPENED?

But something happened over the years of the waning Charismatic movement. Fewer and fewer speakers were actually expressing the Voice. Not many were speaking on the authority that they claimed they were speaking. So the natural responses typical to the Voice also dried up as His Voice was spoken less and less. As the predictable response, there was little to respond to. What started out as genuine, God-breathed responses to His Voice were then being demanded by those speakers who needed the approval of the ones they spoke to.

How many times have we heard, "Do I hear an 'amen'?" or the humorous, but embarrassing, "Hello?" and, "Is anyone out there?"

I want to say, "Yes, we are here. The question is, is there anyone up there at the podium?"

If their words are not the Voice, the genuine "Amen!" will not follow, no matter how often or how convincingly they say, "Thus says the Lord." Believe me, the folks know if it is the Lord by what happens within their own spirits. Where the Voice is spoken and folks are listening, the Lord Jesus within responds with confirming joy. The burden of responsibility is not on the hearers who are expected to respond, it is on the speaker who claims to be proclaiming the Voice. Of course, it is the responsibility of the hearer to be open and listening as well. My emphasis is on the speaker as it is easier to abdicate responsibility to the hearer to hear, even when the Spirit is silent when someone is speaking. I can think of few things more depressing than a speaker talking his own words with no "Amen!" from the Holy Spirit. I personally refuse to enable one who professes to be speaking the word of the Lord when the Lord is not speaking.

No, this Voice cannot be imitated. The anemic voice of man does not stir the heart; does not lift the spirit; does not change a life; convict the sinner or encourage the saint. The voice of man does not build His church, strengthen the weary, heal the sick, restore the soul, or shine as a city on a hill. It does not prepare the saints or gather the brokenhearted. Well did the prophet Jeremiah speak of this generation when he said:

> How can you say, "We are wise, and the law of God is with us"? But behold, the lying pen of the scribes has made it into a lie. The wise men are put to shame, they are dismayed and caught; behold, they have rejected the word of the Lord, and what kind of wisdom do they have? Therefore will I give their wives to others, their fields to new owners; because from the least even to the greatest everyone is greedy

for gain; from the prophet even to the priest every-one practices deceit. They heal the brokenness of the daughter of My people superficially, saying, "Peace, peace," but there is no peace (Jeremiah 8:8-11).

Stuffed with excess and yet we suffer a famine of the word. It is amazing that we live in an age of such diverse and expanding technology and yet God's people still languish. There are an unprecedented number of songs written, books published, and sermons preached. Men use satellites, cable television, radio, the Internet, iPods, iPhones, and iPads. We can stream, download, or log on to any spiritual teaching, conference, missionary work, or Bible school, and yet with all of this at our fingertips, God's people are still broken, scattered, confused, and distraught as ever. Again, Jeremiah peers into today with these words:

"Harvest is past, summer is ended, and we are not saved." For the brokenness of the daughter of my people I am broken; I mourn, dismay has taken hold of me. Is there no balm in Gilead? Is there no physician there? Why then has not the health of the daughter of my people been restored? (Jeremiah 8:20-22)

Is there anyone who loves Him and doubts that this earth needs, no *requires* that we see what He is doing and do the same?

WHICH PLUMB LINE?

When we are busy building our own kingdoms, we tend to look at the church through eyes that are focused on our own four walls. We are satisfied if our little house is in order as we see it. When we are working to maintain what is ours, what goes on around us gives us little concern. Our focus, money, and methods are centered on what is necessary for our own well-being, even our survival.

On the other hand, when we are building His Kingdom, that is, allowing Him to build His Kingdom through us, our focus is much different, for our desire is to see what He is doing and simply do the same thing. His point of view is so different! From His perspective, we see far beyond our own borders, our own needs, our own wants and struggles. The church Jesus is building is a worldwide operation of Jesus living His supernatural life through folks just like us. This is where the real love, the real power, and the real hope bubbles up in the heart of the believer. When we truly see what He is doing—and make no mistake about it, many, many personal kingdom builders do—we have a difficult decision to make. The conflict is valid and the struggle is real. For it is clear that if we build His Kingdom it will be in direct conflict with our own. No one can serve two masters, especially when one of those masters is us.

The Kingdom He is building is the one that few see and even fewer can recognize, for it does not necessarily come with signs and wonders. It does not have the visible attributes that are typical of our own personal monuments. In His Kingdom, He is the center of attention and He gets the glory. In His Kingdom, His purposes prevail and His will is done. The dream He dreams for each of us individually is paramount to His plan. The people who are His church are the very individuals whom so many take for granted and use for their own earthy desires instead of allowing God to do His will.

But it is difficult to want to be a part of what He is doing when it is the opposite of what we are doing. It takes a brave but broken person to build what He is building. There is often little recognition or earthly glory in this. But the peaceable fruit of righteousness cannot be imitated in any way. It produces a state of being in this life that is unmatched any other way. This lifestyle of responding to Him allows His presence to flow like a rushing river out of us to all those around us.

No Visible Signs?

...The kingdom of God is not coming with signs to be observed; nor will they say, "Look, here it is!" or, "There it is!" For behold, the kingdom of God is in your midst (Luke 17:20-21).

The Kingdom of God is the very personal, private work of Jesus in our hearts that urges, convinces, convicts us of sin. It is the very powerful condition of a heart that has learned to submit to Him without argument, fear, or anger. His Kingdom is seen in Spirit in those who have given in to His plans and are learning to quietly give themselves to Him for the purpose of His choosing. It occurs within—without fanfare, fireworks, or the expectation of personal recognition.

But spiritual fireworks are important as they are easily visible in this dimension no matter how spiritually blind one may be to the other dimensions. So let us not hinder the fireworks but not crave them like they are our lifeline, for they most certainly are not.

God-activity is easily recognizable in spirit. For His activity is characterized by supernatural intervention to bring His plan about in time and space. His will always has His stamp on it. That stamp will certainly show an uptick of miraculous activity, but it is much more than that. God-breathed activity is peaceful, even in the midst of sometimes harried activity. The hearts of all involved have a quiet assurance, a peaceful certainty about them. This activity fills the heart with the sweetness of His presence and opens us to the genuine needs around us. The antics of an opportunist leader have no place in this environment. Unfortunately, too many see these supernatural times as a chance to take emotion-filled offerings that bleed the folks or make preposterous promises to those who work, give, or pray the most. God watchers understand that His load is easy and His burden is light. If stress, fear, or intimidation is the rule rather than the exception, I would be wary of it.

THE KINGDOM IS WITHIN AND COMING

When Jesus taught us pray, it was rather simple, although hundreds of volumes have been written about it. I want to show you just one sentence from that prayer. Jesus said, *"Your kingdom come. Your will be done, on earth as it is in heaven"* (Matt. 6:10).

Whatever other reasons Jesus came to earth, He came to build His Father's Kingdom on earth. He has the master plan. His plan, His Kingdom is the only thing that will stand the test of time, trials, and persecution. As a wise master builder who understands what His Kingdom will have to withstand, He builds in everything it will take to come through anything that is thrown against it. Knowing this, why would anyone think that their plan might be better than His? Unless, of course, some do not believe that He means what He says, we all should understand that we need to use His blueprints to build a lasting Kingdom within our hearts.

Those blueprints are simple and easily followed. Love as you want to be loved. Love as God loves you. Forgive, encourage, be patient, gather, heal. In other words, let Jesus truly live His abundant life through you. It makes this life simple and more fulfilling than you can imagine. It also allows you to see Him more clearly without prejudice, limitation, or hesitation. In short, the Kingdom is all about yielding. Yield to God as He wants to love the world through you.

MAN-MADE STRUCTURES WILL FALL

His voice shook the earth then, but now He has promised, saying, "Yet once more I will shake not only the earth, but also the heaven"...so that those things which cannot be shaken may remain" (Hebrews 12:26-27).

When Jesus builds, it remains. It cannot be toppled no matter how hard the shaking may become. This is our hiding place. Those who dwell in Him will not be moved no matter the strength of the shaking. Some miss the point and have not learned to stay put *in Him* when the earthquake comes. We often rebuke the devil so loudly when things are shaking that we cannot hear the Voice of Lord in the thunder. To be sure, "Some heard it thunder," but those with discerning ears know the difference between what is thunder and what is His

Voice. Both can shake the earth. Both are under His control. But only one is the word of eternal life.

There is a time to prevail in prayer. There is a time to stand in the gap between God's plan and anything that is not His plan or something that would disrupt His plan. We will know how to pray as we watch Him to see what He is doing. But it is important that we watch to actually know the difference between what is His activity and what is not. Many times well-meaning believers find themselves fighting God. At times they are trying to break through a wall that just does not seem to want to come down. They fast. They pray. They rebuke. They bind the devil. They claim it. They decree. But at the end of the day, it does not come down. As a result they come to the conclusion that they could not break through the power of the demonic stronghold resisting them. But they failed to realize that perhaps it was Jesus who was resisting them all along. Consider these words of our Lord Jesus:

> ...*I will build My church; and the gates of Hades will not overpower it* (Matthew 16:18).

When man builds his own thing, it is called nothing but wood, hay, and stubble as it is built on a foundation of sand. When He builds something, it is built with precious stones on a solid foundation (Jesus), and cannot be moved. Sometimes we are so sure that something we have built is Him that when the shaking comes we do all that we can to prop it up.

Sometimes God does things that do not agree with our doctrine, our history, our denomination (even if our denomination is non-denominational), or our own plans or ministry dreams. Rather than allowing time to discern whether or not those things are of the Lord, we try to tear them down, or worse, we try to discredit them. Like Gamaliel warned:

> *But if it is of God, you will not be able to overthrow them; or else you may even be found fighting against God* (Acts 5:39).

There is a fine line between working with the Lord and working against Him. The difference is learning to do only what you see Him doing. Of course, even that assumes that you have learned to watch Him.

On the other hand, without watching God, it becomes easy to bless what God is not blessing. In our human intellect, we tend to judge by the outer appearance of things. It takes concerted resolve to wait on the Lord. But in the end, you will be working with Him instead of against Him.

JESUS HAS LEFT THE BUILDING

To be honest, He was never in the building, that is, in brick and mortar buildings. He was and is in us. The church He is building, the church that God watchers are seeing, is vastly different from the ones being constructed on the backs of hard-working, soft-hearted believers who want nothing else but to be found serving Him in the center of His will.

But there is hope! The church as we have defined it, lived it, and financed it is mercifully coming to an end. Jesus Himself is building His church without the advice of man. This church is preparing folks to do His bidding in the secret place of personal tribulation. Do not be afraid; do not wonder if He has left you. He is intricately involved and personally overseeing your transformation into a vessel destined to carry His glory to the nations. Your light, which shines so brightly now, will be seen by more and more as you simply yield to Him who shines through you.

The "city set on a hill" is not a building. It is average folks like you and me who shine with His presence just like a, well, just like a city on a hill.

> *You are the light of the world. A city set on a hill cannot be hidden; nor does anyone light a lamp and put it under a basket, but on the lampstand, and it gives light to all who are in the house. Let your light shine before men in such a way that they may see your good works, and glorify your Father who is in heaven* (Matthew 5:14-16).

Chapter 5

STUCK WHERE WE ARE

THE FIRST WINTER SNOW OF THE SEASON BACK IN 2004 was more exciting than usual around our house. It meant that we could finally take our new Hummer H2 out to test its performance in the snow. I couldn't wait for my sons to come, so I decided to take it around our six acres and run it up a few hills just to break it in before they came. There were about 10 inches (25 centimeters) of snow already on the ground and still snowing very hard. The first test would be a steep hill next to the fencerow on the side of our home. With great anticipation and excitement, I dropped the gear and engaged the four-wheel drive. I started up the hill... for about 10 seconds, when I started sliding and turned sideways and came to rest close to the fence. Not to be deterred, I flipped into one of the six special "get out of a ditch free" gears. The first one did not help. Neither did the next five. By now the Hummer was tight against the fence and almost any movement was going to scratch my new vehicle.

Slightly embarrassed, I called a friend who gladly came with his tractor. One hour later, he was hopelessly stuck as well. As much as I hated to do it, I called my son Matt, who had a big Chevy Dually—a truck with double wheels on each side of the rear. He was very happy to come and pull out his father's Hummer *and* my friend's tractor! His comment was priceless. It had a message I would never forget. Matt said with a big smile, "Dad, one stuck guy cannot pull out another stuck guy." Hummm, so true. Duh.

I began to think about his comment. It is true that over-confidence will always end up getting us stuck, but once we are stuck, we need to find someone who is not stuck and who has the presence of mind and the skill not to get stuck as he helps you!

NO FUN BEING STUCK

There is not a lot of insight in the above statement, for sure. Whether you are stuck in the snow, stuck in the house because you are sick, stuck in a job you don't like, or stuck in the way you believe, being stuck is frustrating. I was going to add that being stuck is also embarrassing, but that is only true if you realize that you are, indeed, stuck!

But I *knew* I was stuck the minute I was no longer moving forward. No kidding. I was spinning my tires but getting nowhere. It is as simple as it is ridiculous—not moving is a definite sign that one is stuck! It reminds me of so many who spin the tires of their Christian experience.

JUST WAIT ANOTHER DAY

It seems as long as we have tomorrow, we have the time to be stuck where we are. Since tomorrow is always the probability of change, I can stay where I am one more day. Too many folks justify waiting to get into a better situation for moving forward simply by putting off the decision that will get them unstuck. It seems so obvious, but making a decision and not acting on it is no decision at all. Yet, many believers are certain that thinking in a certain way is somehow justification in and of itself. But at the end of the day, if nothing is done, nothing is changed by what we think; its impact is negligible at best! The world does not change; we do not change. Hence, it really doesn't matter what anyone believes, so long as they do not act on it. Everything stays the same and we are under no apparent obligation to do anything. Jesus said:

> *Everyone who hears these words of Mine and does not act on them, will be like a foolish man who built his house on the sand. The rain fell, and the floods came, and the winds blew and slammed against that house; and it fell—and great was its fall* (Matthew 7:26-27).

Needless to say, the world is not changed by those who only think righteously, but also by those who act out the righteousness they say they believe. This acting on what we believe certainly not only changes the world, but it also potentially puts these "righteous thinkers" in harm's way when we consider reputation, friendships, and church affiliations. Unfortunately, because of the potential loss involved in truly living what we believe, most are unwilling to pay the price. But there are believers who have always gone forward in spite of the rejection and personal loss they experienced. It is amazing that though they were shunned in life, many of these people are followed and revered in death. The path that many laid is a lifeline for the church Jesus is building.

Yet even though Paul understood this, his passionate love for our Lord led him to pen these most incredible words:

> *But whatever things were gain to me, those things I have counted as loss for the sake of Christ. More than that, I count all things to be loss in view of the surpassing value of knowing Christ Jesus my Lord, for whom I have suffered the loss of all things, and count them but rubbish so that I may gain Christ, and may be found in Him, not having a righteous-ness of my own derived from the Law, but that which is through faith in Christ, the righteousness which comes from God on the basis of faith, that I may know Him and the power of His resurrection and the fellowship of His sufferings, being conformed to His death* (Philippians 3:7-10).

Paul understood that the Kingdom of God does not come by preaching alone, but by stepping into and experiencing the things which we see in Him, things that flow naturally in the Spirit and should flow that freely here in this dimension. These truths are not for another generation. They are not for those special select few who many say are set aside to live this fulfilled Christian life. Paul was driven by desire, hope-ful anticipation that in this life he could attain a strength of relationship that Jesus had with His Father when He walked the earth 2,000 years ago. Hear Paul's heart cry:

> ...but I follow after, if that I may apprehend that for which also I am apprehended of Christ Jesus. Brethren, I count not myself to have apprehended: but this one thing I do, forgetting those things which are behind, and reaching forth unto those things which are before, I press toward the mark for the prize of the high calling of God in Christ Jesus (Philippians 3:12-14 KJV).

THE PRICE OF PROCRASTINATION

But what would happen if we could really see what we lose in Christ by continuously putting off till another day what we know is necessary for us to be a part of God's plan now? I know, I know—it is so difficult to get free of our ruts, those places we have been stuck at for a long time! However, just thinking about being used is not the same as allowing the Lord to actually use you for His service. The *yes* response must passionately overpower the *stuck* factor or we will never move forward. The *yes* must be strong enough to move us to respond to what we say we believe. The world is not changed by folks who think differently; it is changed by those who do something about what they believe.

But there are so many things that keep us tightly locked into what we have always done. There is so much we have been taught that keeps us on a course of another's choosing, rather than one of our choosing or more importantly, His choosing. We have a lifetime of experiences, good and bad, that seem to have control over our actions. These thoughts, beliefs, and experiences will never permit us to change, to experiment, to explore, to grow beyond the safety zone that is subconsciously ruling our lives.

THE DREAM OF GOD

For we are His workmanship, created in Christ Jesus for good works, which God prepared beforehand so that we would walk in them (Ephesians 2:10).

But there is great news—great and encouraging news! God is at work within us. He is completely focused on His plan, His dreams, dare I say, the adventures He has ordained for us. No, you are not in this alone. He is not just waiting somewhere out there for you to stumble upon Him, randomly walking this earth alone. He is proactively at work in your heart so you will grow in courage and hope. He is joining your spirit to His Spirit, your will to His, your mind to the mind of Christ. He is fully expecting a synchronous flow of love between you and Him so there can also be harmonious agreement of His life flowing steadily through you to those around you.

There are plenty of places where we are told about this awesome union with God that we are destined to fulfill in this life. As I said earlier, the Word shows us His nearness so we do not continually wonder where He is. He is near; He is within.

The Spirit itself beareth witness with our spirit, that we are the children of God (Romans 8:16 KJV).

For in Him we live and move and exist... (Acts 17:28).

He shows us that He is at work within, right now.

For it is God who is at work in you, both to will and to work for His good pleasure (Philippians 2:13).

We may not think there is anything positive going on, but He is molding us…right now!

GOD IS NOT SILENT

Today, if you would hear His voice, do not harden your hearts… (Psalm 95:7-8).

Fortunately for us, we do not serve a silent God. We do not serve a God who spoke once thousands of years ago and simply left us to our own humanity to figure things out. He did not return to heaven to tend to a myriad of other pressing universal issues.

God is alive and talking. He is talking to us, to me, to you. In fact, God is a very talkative God. He wants our friendship. He loves to *be* with us. When we are conscious of His presence we *are* with Him. At that point, there is union among the I AMs. He *is* in us and we *are* aware of Him. It is amazing how easy it is for us to forget that God is with us, in us, working, loving, flowing, speaking, singing, dancing, gathering us all to Himself.

We got a glimpse of that when Jesus walked the earth in His physical body. We saw what was done through one person. Although it is good to yield to Him with the goal of doing what Jesus did as He walked the earth, it is important to see that there are yet greater things to be done. Jesus told us there are greater things than He did that are waiting for us to do (see John 14:12). Yielding to Him will bring forth those greater works—actions that we still cannot imagine. Oh, Lord Jesus, teach us to yield so that we can truly see You do more awesome things through Your people!

But many would argue, "He was and is God, no wonder He was able to do such things! If I were God I would do those things too!" But it was not His knowledge of His divinity, but rather the knowledge of His Father's love for Him and for all men that allowed Him to walk in such continuous victory day after day. If He had the "God" advantage, then redemption would have been completed through Him as it was.

> *For we have not an high priest which cannot be touched with the feeling of our infirmities; but was in all points tempted like as we are, yet without sin* (Hebrews 4:15 KJV).

Most would agree that Jesus was the consummate God watcher, but He made it possible for us to become the intentional God watcher that He was. Again, as we see Him, we will more easily yield to His Life flowing through us to the world around us.

SPIRITUAL ABILITY TO HEAR

> *But blessed are your eyes, because they see; and your ears, because they hear. For truly I say to you that many prophets and righteous men desired to see what you see, and did not see it, and to hear what you hear, and did not hear it* (Matthew 13:16-17).

We need the spiritual ability sense spiritual things. We need our spiritual ears open to Him in spite of all the rubbish that tries to dilute and disguise His words to us. If we just had spiritual ability to perceive that He is moving, living, loving all the time, it would change our life's focus. He is real. His activity is real. The dimension from where all this flows is within, where His Kingdom is established.

> *For all the prophets and the Law prophesied until John. And if you are willing to accept it, John himself is Elijah who was to come. He who has ears to hear, let him hear. But to what shall I compare this generation? It is like children sitting in the market places, who call out to the other children, and say, "We played the flute for you, and you did not dance; we sang a dirge, and you did not mourn"* (Matthew 11:13-17).

TODAY, IF YOU HEAR HIS VOICE

> *Therefore, just as the Holy Spirit says, "Today if you hear His voice, do not harden your hearts as when they provoked Me, as in the day of trial in the wilderness, where your fathers tried Me by testing Me, and saw My works for forty years"* (Hebrews 3:7-9).

We should not always wait for a specific spiritual experience, but we should do whatever is in front of us to be done. Our preparation is in our service to Him, within our reach. In fact, they are one and the same. We are prepared as we serve and we serve as we are prepared. They are simultaneous, continuous acts of devotion, our reasonable expectation as we go through life with Him.

Too many folks do not understand the work of the Holy Spirit in preparing us to serve. They are waiting to fulfill a destiny by either doing nothing while they wait or underestimating the power, purpose, or value in what they are doing, as though it is beneath what they should be doing. But what they fail to see is that God is teaching them to serve. God is preparing them for a lifetime of serving. That service, when truly taught by the Holy Spirit, is humble, teachable, patient, and compassionate. When true Brokenness is at work, servants wait for the Lord.

It is in the doing that titles, ministries, callings are truly born. Don't worry about what folks call you. Don't be concerned about recognition or position, for it is God who sees and promotes. The fame among men is fleeting, at best. The recognition attained among men is overrated. We don't have to scrape and crawl over the person in front of us as though we are on our own to achieve God's plan for our lives. There is plenty He puts in front of us to do. There are lots of possibilities to give, serve, and honor Him with our labor of love. He is the only One who really needs to see. Your Father in heaven sees what is done in secret and rewards openly. But for the true God watcher, open reward is not the issue, as they are not driven by the personal accolades of men. Their only desire, satisfaction, and fulfillment is to know they have pleased the Master of their soul. This truly makes life worth living.

THE BRINK OF HUMAN DISASTER

The time will come when we need to respond to what we see Him doing. In truth, we need to be responding right now or we won't be able to respond to the more troubling things tomorrow holds. When we see Him, we are responsible for what we see. When we respond to what we see, we are taking personal responsibility for our actions. Our obedience shows we are taking a road that may not be very popular. We are declaring to the Lord, the world, our friends and colleagues that we are hearing something that is different. We are seeing something we must respond to, something we must do in spite of the dangers, the warnings, as well as the looming possibilities of failure.

These are times of great exhilaration, for sure. We know we have heard Him and the joy, anticipation, and possibilities seem to belie the fear and personal risk if we obey Him. We are a tumult of emotions as we sift through the conflicting feelings that hearing Him inevitably brings to us. At the end of the day, however, no amount of counsel, fasting, and waiting changes the fact that we alone are responsible for what we hear in the secret place of our heart.

If this is where you stand, you are standing at the brink of human disaster. It is the point of exhilaration and dread; ecstatic anticipation and impending doom; the point of no return; here the Jordan parts and you walk into your Promised Land where the real enemies of your soul await your arrival. But it is also the only place your enemies can and will be defeated as you respond to what you see as you watch Him and Him alone. Until you cross the river, the enemies of your soul will dominate your life. They will always be dancing on your destiny, always keeping you short of your Promised Land.

There will be few, indeed, who will agree with your decisions to walk to this brink. To be sure, no one can make that decision for you. It is yours and yours alone. Others can pray for you. They can warn you of potential pitfalls as you move forward. But only God can give you that deep assurance that you are doing the right thing. In the final analysis, you get the glory or the blame for what happens from that moment. The responsibility is squarely and uniquely yours. But that is the exhilaration of doing what you see Jesus doing. That is what makes an adventure a true adventure!

Adventures are by nature trying, to say the least. But knowing you have already seen Him doing it gives you the assurance, the peace to know that you will succeed, even if your success is through many trials. Keep your eyes focused on Him and what you see. The brink of human disaster will turn into a place of success and accomplishment.

Doing what you see your Father doing keeps you on this brink of disaster, but you will never be bored! Life is not dull when you are responding to Him. As He flows through your personality, your life, you watch yourself change as He changes the world through you. It is most exhilarating, if not frightening! Nonetheless, I am learning to love this deeper interaction with Him more than I ever thought I could.

In conclusion, when God watchers respond to what they discover He is doing, they do not evaluate the visibility that their response might gain for them. They do not monetize their response. They are not interested in whether it will help them build their own ministry or reputation. They respond according to the love that it is in their heart. Any other reason reeks of fleshly promotion. Jesus said, "If you have seen Me, you have seen the Father." What transparency! What passion for the work He saw His Father doing! Can ours be

anything less? For certain, this is what changes the world...
today.

This is such an important chapter, because I know so
many, as I am sure you do, who are bitter that they don't have
a "ministry"—meaning they don't have a "titled position" or
recognition of such from "titled people." Meanwhile, there
are plenty of ministry opportunities, right in front of them. A
God watcher, free from the desire for recognition from men,
is too busy "doing" what he sees the Father doing to worry
about whether some people are recognizing it as ministry in
an official capacity. They live before the gaze of One.

Chapter 6

CHILDLIKE VISION OF THE GOD WATCHER

"It's not what you look at that matters, it's what you see." —HENRY DAVID THOREAU

WHAT DO CHILDREN SEE?

SO WHAT DO CHILDREN SEE? CHILDREN *SEE* THE SAME THINGS adults see. It is their *perception* of what they see that made Jesus warn:

> *"Permit the children to come to Me; do not hinder them; for the kingdom of God belongs to such as these. Truly I say to you, whoever does not receive the kingdom of God like a child will not enter it at all." And He took them in His arms and began*

blessing them, laying His hands on them (Mark 10:14-16).

Children have the same eyes as adults, but they process what they see through an innocence that adults have unfortunately lost a long, long time ago. I love listening to my grandkids for that very reason. Their discussions among themselves are more than cute, they are enlightening. Most of you have probably heard a few four year olds in deep conversation. Their perspectives are unique only because they are so innocent. They believe everything and everyone. They have no reason to mistrust a stranger with candy. They do not hesitate to repeat what they heard their folks say in the privacy of their own home. They assume that what they hear at school, on the playground, or on the Internet is true. We actually think we have to teach the innocence out of them for their own well-being. How sad that is.

Maturity is innocence with divine discernment, bathed in God's love.

> *Brethren, do not be children in your thinking; yet in evil be infants, but in your thinking be mature* (1 Corinthians 14:20).

To learn discernment while maintaining the innocence of heart that allows God to show us His place in everything is the key to childlikeness, without which, as we have discovered, we will not experience His Kingdom in this life.

It is quite impossible to be a God watcher if there is not this divine duality at work in us. We need to have the willingness to see through the eyes of a child, where everything is new, innocent, exciting, and wonderful. But with child-like vision, we also need the discernment to separate the pure from the vile—those things that appear to be pure but carry destruction within their hearts.

Unfortunately, this process still requires vulnerability, something many are not willing to subject themselves to—and with good reason. We know where vulnerability often leads. Nonetheless, Brokenness requires that we make decisions that will cause us to be a target for many. But the opportunity to co-labor with our Lord in His purposes for earth is worth more than whatever man may do to us.

It takes focused determination not to be jaded by the things that try to force us to give up our innocence rather than remain true to the One to whom we have given our heart. As I said earlier, *innocence* needs to be defined in the context of what Jesus said when He referred to little children. I am happy to be called *childlike*. Some who have no idea what this innocence in Christ is all about will go so far as to call me *immature*. But this kind of challenge is so good! It causes me to check my heart and look carefully at the plumb line of Jesus. He always helps me see if am still living in innocence that allows me to see Him as He really is—free, pure, loving, giving with overpowering mercy, compassion, and grace.

MY CHILD TAUGHT ME

The very first major worship conference of contemporary times was held at the Marriott in Orlando, Florida in 1988. In those days, Charismatic, full-Gospel books were very scarce as few main-line publishers would risk the stigma of publishing "those kinds of books." So this time around, it was Matt's turn to go with me and help set up our book display. He was only eight, but was still great company and a big help too! With five sons, they all took turns traveling with me. Someone seemed to be out of school a couple times a month. What they learned over those impressionable years traveling with me is far more than we can calculate. They work in the ministry today partially due to those times. But they were not the only ones to learn, and I was not the only teacher, as this trip proved.

We had driven from Pennsylvania, a trip of about fifteen hours. When the time came to set up our booth, we discovered an avalanche of vendors pressing on the lone manager in charge. Although we had been promised the prime spot due to the distance we traveled and the size of our display, others were setting their booths where we were to have ours. I immediately got more than a little upset with the turn of events. I was about to express my displeasure to that harried manager when I felt a tug on my pant leg. I looked down to see Matt's smiling face. Beaming from ear to ear, he said simply, "Dad, let's go back to the room and just trust God." What? Was this my son? I knew that it was more than his own light shining on me as he spoke. God was talking to me and I had better listen. We returned to the conference site two hours later to find our spot, exactly where promised, waiting for us. Matt turned to me, again with that contagious smile and said while shaking his little head, "See, God always takes care of us!"

I looked at him and smiled back, "He sure does, son. He sure does."

I am discovering that God uses everything around us to show Himself to us. He will use a small child, sometimes a movie, sometimes even Oprah. I am absolutely certain He will use an ass. Just sayin'—He uses me.

THE CHILDLIKE ARE TEACHABLE

Whoever then humbles himself as this child, he is the greatest in the kingdom of heaven. And whoever receives one such child in My name receives Me (Matthew 18:4-5).

Of course, the degree to which we can be taught by others is directly related to the time we spend with Brokenness, who replaces pride with humility, agitation with peace, and judgment with true love. The degree to which we recognize everyone around us as a potential teacher is directly related to our opinion of ourselves. The greater we see ourselves, the fewer there will be who can show us anything.

God is a prolific talker. His very nature is revelatory to us humans. He has a lot to say. Brokenness teaches me to listen to Him rather than to myself or others, even when they are well-meaning. Until I see myself clearly, it is certain that my thoughts, my opinions, my interpretations are far more important than anyone else's. My picture is quite skewed—I am a giant among men in my own eyes. I am a figment of my own imagination.

Dear Jesus, keep me small in my own eyes that I may learn of Your greatness from everyone around me!

HIGH WIRE ACT OR YIELD TO HIM

The balance is such a fine line. On the one hand, so many voices, including our own, try to keep us contained, keep us from saying what we see in His heart. They belittle, scoff, accuse, and downright lie to us. We must resist those voices. But those same voices can also inflate our ego, make us seem to be God's gift to the earth—like all of God's purposes waited for our appearance on the earth and now that we are here, He can finally come. Ha! Unregenerate humanity will always wander into pride.

The balance is known only to Brokenness, who will keep us steady. Balance is not in a man; it is not a ministry for a well-meaning brother or sister in Christ. God will often use others, but the ones I listen to are the ones with whom I am close friends, those who have my best interests at heart and who know I have their best interests at heart. I listen to those with whom I shared the crucible of trial. I want the truth, but I want the truth by one whom I know loves me.

At the end of the day, I am one who is glad the balance is in the church Jesus is building, not in the individual believer. That way I am free to respond to God as He carefully weaves me through the ins and outs of knowing how to live and how to respond to Him.

HOW DO WE WATCH HIM?

A disciple is not above his teacher, nor a slave above his master. It is enough for the disciple that he become like his teacher, and the slave like his master... (Matthew 10:24-25).

The miracles of the Master got the attention of those who saw Him do these great supernatural acts, but it was the way He lived, spoke, and loved that showed the world that He was and is the Son of God. The fruit of what the disciple does also defines who he is. The things that a disciple does may get folks' attention, but the Spirit in which he lives defines who he really is in his heart. When the man's actions neither match the words he says nor reflect the miracles he performs, his credibility is lost, sometimes forever. That is not to say the disciples are perfect. To be sure, true disciples are more aware of their failures than anyone else, and it pains them that sometimes their actions may skew another's view of who God really is. At the end of the day, it is not the miracles that God wants folks to see. God wants them to see *Himself in you.*

This awareness of personal weakness keeps His disciples small in their own eyes, humble when talking to others, and repentant when they are before God. They are aware of just how real God is and are nearly destroyed by their awareness of their own humanity. This is truly Brokenness. His disciples want nothing more than to be an accurate representation of their Lord to the world. Nothing else matters. They know that when the world really sees Jesus, folks will run to Him.

It is amazing that we are so concerned with signs and wonders returning to the church but do not give as much emphasis on character. It is as though we do not realize that true godly power flows through love and compassion. We have all kinds of excuses for why all those we pray for are not healed. For now, we may not be able to see everyone healed as we would like to. We do not control God, so we cannot predict what will really happen when we pray, although we have all learned enough religious slang to cover the emptiness of our hands and the uncertainty of our hearts.

But there is one thing that is completely under our control. Our will and emotions play a much greater role in our daily walk with God than we have imagined. I do not want to get into that discussion right now; suffice it to say that we need to allow our Lord to so freely love through us that He is able to do all He wants to do through us without hindrance. When pure love flows freely, God's will is done. Pure love flows through a broken and contrite heart—a childlike heart. All He is flows right now through His people. But we are too easily distracted with the things of this dimension that we miss the moment reality of His dimension that flows continuously through us.

WATCHING MAN

...and all of you, clothe yourselves with humility toward one another, for God is opposed to the proud, but gives grace to the humble (1 Peter 5:5).

There is much we can learn from one another, and a childlike heart is always willing to be taught. Those who walked before us have wisdom that can save us years of heartache and suffering if we are humble enough to learn from them. I love to visit with men and women who have been in the "trenches." I listen carefully to them, watch them, and learn from their example. Sometimes I learn from their mistakes too. In fact, their mistakes are essential to understand and analyze. The way I look at it, why should I suffer for a lesson that someone else already suffered for? Unfortunately, I do not do that often enough, so I go through the same learning curve (or should I say *suffering curve*) that many others have. Our nature can be so stubborn.

But it is the nature of our humanity. We don't seem to get it unless we ourselves suffer for it. Life would be much easier if we would just learn by hearing, rather than learning by failing. That's why real maturity is more profound than we normally imagine. When we finally get to the point where we have learned to heed the warnings, advice, and failures of others, we are truly growing. Changing actions in response to instruction rather than failure saves us time and pain. It will ultimately catapult us much further into all God has dreamed for us.

Think of the children of Israel. Had they believed God, taken His counsel through Moses, they would have had a straight shot through the wilderness. But as we all know, they suffered forty years until they finally got the message and obeyed in spite of their fears.

The older I get, the more I realize that years do not produce wisdom—Brokenness produces wisdom. I am ashamed to think of how many three-part sermons I wrote simply out of my own wisdom, while being positive it was God's wisdom. But Brokenness teaches us to yield to Him, no matter what He says, even when He says nothing. Yes, that's right, sometimes He says nothing. When we need to remain silent, He is also silent. But we are far too "spiritual" to accept that. We just "press in," assuming that He can't possibly have nothing for us to say or do in a particular situation. It is a hard lesson, but most of us can preach, counsel, lead out of our soulish heart much more easily than waiting for Him, especially when He speaks by being silent.

Yes, if the years have taught me anything, it is that the years don't teach us. He teaches us in the crucible of failure, struggle, and pain. Unfortunately, the folks closest to us are tools of change, but this is when we learn there is only Christ and He is our everything. We can be angry or we can be changed; the decision is completely ours. But if we choose to be angry, that lesson will come around again until we get it. I am so dense, though. Sometimes a lesson has to come around again and again before I get it. Thank God for His patience.

I regret having spent so much time wandering short of His dreams, instead of learning the lessons I needed to learn in order to do all He has for me. What I could have learned from others would have changed my life's course long ago.

> Lord, please give me a heart to hear, humility to accept what You say, and the courage to walk it out, no matter who You decide to use as the catalyst for my change!

My goal is to live a repentant and transparent life before God and a humble and loving and forgiving life before man. This is getting easier as I see my complete bankruptcy without Him. If He does not condemn me, how can I possibly condemn another?

> For thus says the high and exalted One who lives forever, whose name is Holy, "I dwell on a high and holy place, and also with the contrite and lowly of

spirit in order to revive the spirit of the lowly and to revive the heart of the contrite" (Isaiah 57:15).

I have heard something very clear and very hopeful deep in my spirit. There is nothing God wants more than to express Himself fully through the likes of a simple person like me. His plan is all about bringing this to pass in the *now*. He allows this flow in direct proportion to my willingness to lay down myself, with all that means, and simply yield. Once again, no one said it better than John the Baptizer, "He must increase; I must decrease."

Chapter 7

THE RISE OF THE
GOD WATCHERS

WHEN JESUS ROSE FROM THE DEAD, HE OPENED THE DOOR for all to join His order of priests, the priesthood of Melchizedek. This is a mysteriously wonderful, enchanting priesthood that ushers all who call Jesus their Lord into an incredible lifestyle, first introduced to us by Jesus Himself as He walked the earth. The priests in this order carry the love, reality, and dreams of God Himself in their hearts.

The priesthood is named after the first priest of this New Covenant order. He made his brief appearance to Abraham, our father in faith. Here is some of what the Scripture says about Melchizedek.

> *For this Melchizedek, king of Salem, priest of the Most High God, who met Abraham as he was returning from the slaughter of the kings and blessed him, to whom also Abraham apportioned a tenth*

part of all the spoils, was first of all, by the translation of his name, king of righteousness, and then also king of Salem, which is king of peace. Without father, without mother, without genealogy, having neither beginning of days nor end of life, but made like the Son of God, he remains a priest perpetually. Now observe how great this man was to whom Abraham, the patriarch, gave a tenth of the choicest spoils (Hebrews 7:1-4).

The Bible says that Melchizedek was a priest:

…not on the basis of a law of physical requirement, but according to the power of an indestructible life. For it is attested of Him, "You are a priest forever according to the order of Melchizedek" (Hebrews 7:16-17).

Because Jesus lead the way for us, we too are in this priesthood:

But you are a chosen race, a royal priesthood, a holy nation, a people for God's own possession… (1 Peter 2:9).

Most of us have barely begun to discover all that it means to be a priest like Jesus, in the order of Melchizedek. But it is God's intention for us to discover, experience, and continually walk in this eternal priesthood. God watchers discover who they are and all they can experience in this priesthood.

You have made them to be a kingdom and priests to our God; and they will reign upon the earth (Revelation 5:10).

WHO DO WE LISTEN TO?

For now we see in a mirror dimly, but then face to face; now I know in part, but then I will know fully just as I also have been fully known (1 Corinthians 13:12).

True God watchers refine their vision moment to moment. They rarely take another's view for granted, guarding their hearts and spirits carefully. They do not ignore others. Quite the contrary, God watchers understand that we are all potentially, if not in reality, God watchers. Every believer has eyes to see if he chooses to look. If we are to get the full picture of all He is, we need to be willing to be taught by all around us. Remember, we are all in the priesthood of Melchizedek.

God, after He spoke long ago to the fathers in the prophets in many portions and in many ways, in these last days has spoken to us in His Son, whom He appointed heir of all things, through whom also He made the world. And He is the radiance of His glory and the exact representation of His nature... (Hebrews 1:1-3).

This Scripture explains that Jesus is the exact mirror of His Father. But it goes beyond what we call a "mirror image," for Jesus was the exact representation of His Father by nature. No wonder the Scriptures record this conversation:

Philip said to Him, "Lord, show us the Father, and it is enough for us." Jesus said to him, "Have I been so long with you, and yet you have not come to

know Me, Philip? He who has seen Me has seen the
Father...” (John 14:8-9).

The question is not so much who is allowed to see Him, but rather will we allow ourselves to see Him for who He really is. To allow ourselves to see Him and then allow Him to live His life through us can be a frightening prospect. Most certainly, we will find ourselves doing things we would not otherwise do, probably things we would not want to do— love the ones we don't want to love; forgive those we don't want to forgive; see as He changes our attitudes, desires, and outlook on life itself. Yes, seeing Him for who He really is changes everything. There is no doubt that it is only by His Spirit that we can change at all. Teachers can teach us all day, but they will never change our hearts unless they speak the words that the Holy Spirit wills to chisel onto our hearts, because they are God's words.

> *As for you, the anointing which you received from*
> *Him abides in you, and you have no need for anyone*
> *to teach you; but as His anointing teaches you about*
> *all things, and is true and is not a lie, and just as*
> *it has taught you, you abide in Him* (1 John 2:27).

THE SUPERNATURAL ORDER OF THINGS

It is God's plan for all of us to see Him, recognize Him, and allow Him to live His glorious life through the likes of simple folks like you and me. At the end of the day, the five-fold ministry of Ephesians 4:11 is responsible to teach the saints to hear God for themselves, to yield to Him, to respond to Brokenness, and to obey Him as He flows through us for all the world to see. When this happens, the saints are equipped to go out and equip others as they have been prepared. This is the natural order, or should I say the supernatural order of things.

The five-fold ministry does not exist in the Most Holy Place. Its function is in the Holy Place, where believers are equipped and brought to the discovery of who they really are. Then they are released to change their world as they are led. Some may become five-fold ministers and some will not, but all will graduate—in God's timing, not man's—into the fullness of God's dream for them.

So it is critical that we see real, God-breathed life beyond the five-fold ministry. God has not hidden His truth from all but a select group. Certainly they carry a burden and responsibility that is commensurate with their office, but that does not mean the rest of the Body does not possesses the ability and responsibility to hear for themselves. These essential ministries are vital for their role in giving the church Jesus is building the necessary tools to hear and respond to their Lord personally. Discipline, sensitivity, and softness of heart are nurtured so that the Body can hear the Lord for themselves.

However, there is so much being done to establish these the five-fold ministries in the church that there seems to be a disconnect between these ministries and the true equipping and sending of those who are to be prepared. Just like all the movements of the past, some in power are working to cement their base while those who do an equally essential work in the trenches of the church are often left unnoticed, unprepared, uncared for, and unappreciated. But the Melchizedek priesthood, the universal priesthood of all believers in Jesus, has a function that leaders must understand. For the purposes of God will not be fulfilled until the church Jesus is building has the strength, love, unity, and coordination to stand upright, automatically raising the Head, even Jesus, up so all men can be drawn to Him.

The priesthood of Melchizedek, which is the priesthood of the believer, is alive and well. The work of the five-fold ministry is to prepare the believer into their calling. Nothing can stop this priesthood that carries His presence within them. Hell itself could not stop the Christ of God, and it cannot stop Him now as He shows Himself mighty to save, heal, deliver, love, and gather through the likes of simple folks like you and me.

TRUE LEADERSHIP EQUIPS THE SAINTS

The true leaders are those who equip to send, really releasing the folks to do the will of God with no strings attached. They have no responsibility but to love and no agenda but to see the true Body of Christ emerge unhindered, unrestrained, and only under the Lordship of Jesus. These true leaders understand that they equip to release. Their goal is not establish a monetary base from those they send, but to establish a spiritual Bride through whom Jesus can truly live His life, release His love, and grow His Kingdom.

Remember that authority is never assigned, it must be earned; never assumed, it is embraced; never forcing itself on others, but always leading by example.

Just like the movements of the past, this leadership movement will eventually find its proper place in the Body of Christ. The saints will move forward with love and conviction, assuming their willingness to find their proper place in the overall restoration of the life of Christ in our hearts. While pastors, who are the unsung heroes of the church Jesus is building, continue their moment by moment work of caring for the saints, His plan will go forward. Those who now identify themselves as five-fold ministries must discover their true role in the process of working among the churches in harmony with the true purposes of God and under His Lordship. If they fail to find their God-ordained place, they will become irrelevant and a whole new generation of broken and teachable five-fold ministries will need to emerge.

In the meantime, be patient, saint of God. You will discover that there is real hope in the emergence of genuine five-fold ministries in this movement as there was in the worship, prophetic, destiny, and kingdom movements. The true church Jesus is building is moving ever closer to the real calling and passion of our Lord Jesus. The true nature of the Body of Christ will be recognized in those who really carry the passion of the Lord. For there is no greater reward than doing what you are called to do, with or without the approval of anyone. There is no greater ordination than the one the Lord bestows upon His people. They are committed to live in the "yes" of God even if they are hearing "no" from those who are supposed to be preparing them.

THE INTERCESSION OF THE GOD WATCHER

As a Melchizedek priest I carry the birth pangs of spiritually birthing the Christ Child within myself personally and the Body of Christ at large. When these come upon me, I try to get alone and yield to them, rather than fight them or try to understand them. I try to relax, pray in the Spirit, groan, pray in English, or respond however it feels good to respond. Childbirth is out of our control both naturally and spiritually. I usually teach that the spirit of the Prophet is subject to the prophet. This is still true concerning childbirth. In the natural, you yielded to union which resulted in a child. In the Spirit, we also yield to union with our Creator. The result is the Son of God being formed within us individually and corporately. Our birth pangs are the signal that the birth is near. The reality is, though, we give birth many times as we mature in Him and in our destiny. We can intercede and birth Christ within ourselves, other people, nations, believers, or non-believers. Spiritual birth pangs come as a matter of course to those who yield thusly to union with their Creator.

God watchers are sober in what they see, how they speak, and what they do. They have laid aside the tags that believers wear as an honor or display to cement their authority. They see that there is no time for such antics. When they see God, their passion is the unwavering intercession that brings what they see into time and space. They know that God's activity within, among, and around His people is the only hope for the world. Their prayer life often causes them to appear distant, almost disconnected from the activity around them. But that is usually because they are connected with the other-world power that God is pouring through them.

But don't get me wrong—God watchers are not flaky. They are absolutely connected to this dimension as well as the dimension of the Spirit. In the early days of the "Charis-maniac" movement, folks were often described as being so spiritual that they were no earthly good. Folks who were labeled this way considered it a badge of honor. It was considered OK to be strange, detached, or otherwise weird. But I do not know of anyone more heavenly minded than Jesus. Yet He was also the most earthly good.

It is certain that Jesus spent an incredible amount of time in prayer—that is, in direct communion with His Father. But that communion took place, for the most part, in the solitude of His prayer closet. What They talked about is mostly a mystery except for a few glimpses we have scattered throughout the Gospels, most notably John 17. But when He was with the people, He was always engaged with them. He sensed their needs, their thoughts, their pain, and their hopes. He gave Himself to the people without the appearance of the weirdness of so many today who have to prove their spirituality by the "different" ways they act and speak. The religious folks hated Him for sure, but it was not because of His strange ways. They hated Him because they knew Jesus was a threat to their very existence; He carried truth with sober certainty and ministered life with unwavering consistency. His words made sense. They convicted the religious and the sinner alike. When the Pharisees would discredit Him, Jesus healed their sick and preached freedom to the captives. This One could not be easily dismissed as a madman. Everything about Him confirmed Truth that could not be disputed. The only thing they could do to Him was murder Him. You will know you are reaching the nerves of those around you when they no longer dismiss you as an angry lunatic, but start planning your serious discreditation.

FASTEN YOUR SEAT BELTS

Everything we know about church, doctrine, and faith is changing. There is no stopping it. If I don't say it, there are thousands, maybe millions who are seeing, hearing the same things I am saying. As Jesus said so long ago when He was asked to stop the people from singing His praise, "If they keep quiet, the rocks will sing out" (see Luke 19:40). This is not anything new, but it is a renewal of everything that has already been said, everything that was first revealed when Jesus walked the earth. The appearance of our faith is having a face-lift, a renewing, a real live experience of Jesus in a way that can only be experienced.

I cannot stop this change, this evolution. I cannot control it. I can only report on what I see for the days to come. I am watching Him. He is looking for folks with existing platforms to be the voices of change, the cries for renewal, and in many instances, for revolution. But if they refuse to say what they see, our Lord will not quit; He will again look to the streets. The greatest harvest fields are among those with nothing to lose and everything to gain. They are ones God will use, for they are willing.

If we can somehow maintain this same attitude, we will always be relevant to His plan. For the rising of His Presence among men will not be exclusive to a denomination or stream. It won't happen just among young people, a current movement, a person, or a television show. It is coming to all who will respond to Him, all who will be under His Lordship. These folks are coming—without titles, flamboyant meetings, or gaudy posters proclaiming something they had nothing to do with. Any individual claiming ownership of what God is about to do will ultimately be sidelined by their arrogance and personal kingdom building.

The Lordship of Jesus as demonstrated in His people will prevail, whether it is reported by the Christian media or published in Christian books. He will build His own church. It will be as obvious as a city on a hill, as compassionate as healing on the Sabbath, as selfless as giving one's life for His friends, and as powerful as divine resurrection. It will be as quiet as talking to a trusted friend, as confident as rebuilding a temple in three days as Jesus said He would do. The church Jesus is building is as humble as kneeling with a prostitute and as passionate as cleansing the temple grounds. This church will multiply food, not just to show His power but to feed the hungry. The church Jesus is building will raise the dead, not show off His power but to give life to a friend. He will heal a bleeding woman for no other reason than to show His love to the weakest of all among us. His people will preach the Kingdom of God to create a throne within us, not because it is a good church attendance program.

THE MINISTRY OF THE CHURCH JESUS IS BUILDING

This is who will prevail, this is whom He will use—the broken, the rejected, the compassionate, the needy, the small, the weak, the hidden. All these will change the world, proclaim His coming, and see Him every day. With their eyes upon Him, these then will understand the secrets of His Kingdom. They experience what cannot be seen, know what cannot be told, and sense what can only be described as righteousness, peace, and joy in the Holy Spirit. If there is an end to this era, it will be the church that Jesus Himself is building that ushers it in, without personal fanfare, recognition, and without the need or even the thought of the praise of men.

I have said this a thousand times. His church is built by His hands alone; His Kingdom comes at His command alone. The only visible one will be Him. He alone determines the details of His plan, which, to be sure, is none of our business until He chooses to reveal it to those broken enough to receive it without using it for personal gain or notoriety.

ESTABLISHING HIS IDENTITY

A God watcher knows that it doesn't matter what man calls us or even what he sees in us. The real question will always be, "Do the people we are ministering among see Him in us?" My focus is never on what others think, feel, or believe about me. I am a follower of Jesus. I am not a sideshow attraction for someone's circus. I do not answer to the three-ring barker under the big top. My focus is deliberate, serious, constant, single-minded, and unshakable. I yield so He can shine. All other self-proclaiming goals or accomplishments are a waste of time. If I am to be promoted, recognized, or otherwise seen, that is His business, not mine. My passion is always what is in front of me, within my reach right now. What is far off is out of my reach. When He leads me there, I will continue to do what I have always done—bless, love, heal, give, encourage, forgive, gather to His throne. With that as my attitude, His Voice is spoken with the clarity, compassion, encouragement, love, and power that will change both me and those whom I touch.

I see myself as a lamp for Him, shining His glorious light that gives man hope. That works fine for me. I am not so glorious, so whatever folks see in me that reminds them of my Lord is definitely His light shining. I carry His presence throughout my life in this dimension of time and space. When Jesus calls me home, I am fulfilled in that whilst I lived I did my best to yield to Him so the world could see Him in me and through me. If I do that to best of my ability, I will have done God's will.

Chapter 8

THE DISCERNMENT OF THE GOD WATCHER

THE PRIESTHOOD OF THE BELIEVER

GOD WATCHERS UNDERSTAND THAT THE HOPE OF THE WORLD is to see the entire Body of Christ committed and trained to be God watchers. As you know by now, God watching is the responsibility of everyone, because we are all in the priesthood of the believer, Melchizedek. There is no one dismissed from the responsibility to be a God watcher, which is, in reality, godly discernment. If you are truly watching God, your heart is yearning for the maturing of the whole Body of Christ.

Paul understood this and labored with all his strength to see the maturing of the Body of Christ. The cry of his heart was that everyone would become a God watcher.

For the anxious longing of the creation waits eagerly for the revealing of the sons of God (Romans 8:19).

Now this is a refreshing attitude to have toward one another. Paul knew that the hope of the world was not in his title. The world's hope is in the church Jesus is building to discover the fullness of God within for themselves. He knew that the individual believer as well as the corporate Body holds the key to all God has planned for this planet. Because he knew this, Paul prayed for those he ministered to. He knew he was co-laboring with God. He knew that God's plan was intrinsic to his relationship with the people he served. Paul knew that God *expected* him to teach the folks exactly what he saw God doing. He did not have the right to use God's people for his own personal gain and goals.

This selfless commitment to God's people is one that is the leading passion of all God watchers. One cannot separate God's plan from His people and expect that God's plan will be accomplished anyway. We do not live in a spiritual vacuum. God's direction is not something we can take or leave. We are here to do His bidding among His people and all the peoples of the earth.

Yet, the God watcher is burdened that many do not seem to understand this. It is hard to tell whether some do not see their own worth in His plan, or perhaps they do not believe that God even has a plan. It may also be that they do not know what God is up to. It might even be that they are not accustomed to divine revelation or seeing the Lord at work in their lives. But God's heart and attention is constantly toward His people. He will show them that He is so intimately involved in their lives.

Paul's prayer and the God watcher's prayer is that all would come to the fullness of the knowledge of Jesus, to a mature man, to the stature of the measure that belongs to the fullness of Christ. Paul was not looking to secure his future income or his reputation; he wanted the will of God done in his life and in the lives of those entrusted to him by God, and he ministered, he gave of himself passionately to that end.

The true God watcher is not watching God just for himself, but for all those he is privileged to touch in his lifetime. His words encourage, plant hope, show compassion, speak the truth in love, and heal. In short, the words of God watchers point to Jesus Himself. Their words reflect the fruit of the Spirit and paint a brushstroke of who God is. Remember that the stroke of a paintbrush is made up of hundreds of individual bristles that are together painting the same stroke. The more folks there are watching Him, the more clearly His person, activity, and plan can be seen and done. It does not matter how clearly we may see something in the Spirit, it takes the Body to bring it into time and space. Unless what God has done in the Spirit comes into our dimension, it will not do what it is intended to do.

GOD WATCHERS BEGET GOD WATCHERS

Those who build according to their personal and private agenda do not want the folks who follow them to understand the workings of God for themselves. They prefer to surround themselves with people who are *not* God watchers. If the believer could discern the work of His Kingdom from the sweaty works of mere mortal man, who operates using the Name of Jesus but does not live in the Name of Jesus, things would be quite different. In short, personal agenda builders build their own thing hoping that it looks enough like His thing that no one will notice the difference.

In contrast, the God watcher covets the true Christ-centered discernment of others who walk with him. The true Kingdom builder surrounds himself with the wise and discerning, for they are not interested in maintaining a power base or personal cash flow. He understands that the more people understand Him and know what He is building, the better off the whole Body of Christ will be. The true God watcher is also painfully aware that his own discernment fails at times and so he is deeply aware of his need for others in the Body of Christ. Our hope is not in one person who can see the whole plan of our Lord. Our hope is in the many-membered Body who sees and confirms and sometimes does not see and warns. We are all in this together. Sometimes we forget that we are co-laborers, not competitors.

> For we know in part and we prophesy in part; but when the perfect comes, the partial will be done away. When I was a child, I used to speak like a child, think like a child, reason like a child; when I became a man, I did away with childish things. For now we see in a mirror dimly, but then face to face; now I know in part, but then I will know fully just as I also have been fully known (1 Corinthians 13:9-12).

RELEASED TO BE FREE

I can remember when I fell in love with Cathy. All apparent reason went out the window. I was in love. My life was focused, lopsided, and unpredictable as I pursued her day by day. I would not rest until I had her. Now, over forty years, five children, and lots of bumps and bruises later, lots of things have changed in our relationship, but we are more in love now than ever before. We enjoy each other's company, laughter, and friendship in a way I would never have been able to predict, simply because I did not know this level of relationship was even possible. Love changed everything and still changes everything. My love for her constantly redefines my life in relation to her and causes our union to be not just physical as it was in the beginning, but a genuine spiritual oneness.

My relationship with God can also be equally defined. Mere intellectual argument will never be enough to change my core beliefs, no matter where they come from. Otherwise I would be no more than an aimless ship being driven by whatever wind happens to be blowing at the moment. On the other side, there are so many hungry people and so few true God watchers that their hunger drives them to catch any wind, any word, any spirit that comes along. I do not completely blame these hungry folks. That is why we all should become God watchers in whatever place we are called to be, whatever we do every day. These hungry saints must be able to see through those who do not really have their best interests at heart. On the other hand, those who flippantly carry grandiose titles as though they are the ones to follow will have more to answer for than they can possibly imagine. It is as though some either think that God does not see them or that He does not care. It is as though these title-bearers do not see that they have an eternal responsibility for their generation, not to secure their own place in religious history or even their own income and retirement.

The believer, although already a priest of the Melchizedek order, still needs to be discipled and released into the calling that God has given him. Although we are born into this awesome priesthood, we will truly function effectively in it as we mature. It is the nature of immature believers to gravitate to those who are in the forefront to validate them, love them, shepherd them as the Great Shepherd does so they can do what burns in their hearts to do, no matter what that may be. As we mature, we can be more confident that what burns within is born of Him. I do not want to be one who carries a weighty title without the God-breathed calling to carry out what that office requires. In the last analysis, our interpersonal relationship with people is what allows the miracle of transformation to occur in everyone.

It is important that we do not fear the word *discipleship*, as misused as it has been over the years. For there is nothing more validating, nothing more powerful than genuine love among God's people. Those who are locked in the destiny of God by genuine agape love will see themselves blossom into all He has dreamed for them to be. These are the leaders who have the best interests at heart for the folks they care for. There is no fear in love that is born of God and no fear in counsel born of Brokenness. Everyone needs the discernment to decide to whom they will entrust their soul. This kind of respect does not come with title, popularity, talent, or even calling. It is earned in the day-to-day trenches of relationship.

The question remains, who will show God's people the ways of their Lord? Who will lay down their own lives that those to whom they are called will flourish in the plan of God? Who is willing to remain in the shadows so the light of the glory of God may shine through the faces of those called to change the world?

THE DISCERNMENT OF A GOD WATCHER

As a God watcher, I discern who I will align myself with; I want to know if their heart is tied to His. I want to be sure that their passion is to do the will of God. Since I am responsible for my time, finances, and family, I want to be sure I am working with those who walk as I do.

I do not live my life questioning and examining everything that goes on around me. But I am sensitive to the Holy Spirit within. When He catches my attention, I know that there is something going on that I need to be aware of. Especially when there is no outward or obvious evidence to catch my attention. His presence within either warning or affirming is enough to cause me to trust what I feel over what my five senses are telling me.

So be careful not to run from your feelings. While it is true that there are many who have not been able to separate the soul from the spirit, many more are learning to successfully navigate the complex inner workings of our beings and are able to know the difference.

GOD WATCHERS ARE SLOW TO SPEAK

Our discernment is not only critical to our well-being, but also to our ability to know what is God's plan and what is not. It makes me so careful to sense strongly what God is doing before I will open my mouth.

> *Let not many of you become teachers, my brethren,*
> *knowing that as such we will incur a stricter judg-*
> *ment* (James 3:1).

It is amazing the way words flow so freely from our mouths with the confidence and assurance that we are speaking the very words of our Lord to the people. Much of the time, we are speaking out of our soul trying to secure our own position among them. I wonder if those who are prone to exploiting or controlling others by prophesying or teaching so easily realize how they test Him, how thin the ice is they are actually walking on. Maybe it's just me, but that deception for personal gain is just frightening to me. I know Him. I know He is real. I know that He is attuned to what I say. I know His people are the apple of His eye. I also know that one does not mess with God's special treasure.

I remember some instruction I got from an important "apostolic" ministry. "Never tell the people everything you know. It will keep them coming back. Besides, if you tell them too much, they may advance beyond you." I can honestly report to you that I rejected that advice the moment I heard it. I cannot imagine not giving everything I know, everything I have, and everything I am so that God's people can grow.

I have had that attitude with my five sons as well. Cathy and I gave them every opportunity to grow physically, emotionally, and spiritually. We let them ask a million questions. And they did! For the most part, we tried to give them the best answers we had or told them outright we did not know the answer, but we could look for the answer together. We wanted our sons to grow and go far beyond everything we could ever have accomplished. We are watching them do that now. It is a great blessing, indeed!

TEACHING DISCERNMENT TO CHILDREN

As I said, our children were not shielded by much as they grew up. Shielding children is like a tree growing in such a protected environment that it is not able to withstand the storms when they are out with no protection. Of course, we were careful what they were exposed to, but we also taught them discernment in the midst of a song, a movie, an argument they saw at a restaurant, etc. Our goal was to have them grow up to be wise in the ways of the adversary as well as keen to discern his diabolical activity in any circumstance.

It may not be our responsibility to judge another's actions, but we had better know how to respond to protect those around us when we see something that we know would be harmful to ourselves, our families, or anyone else who looks to us for help, guidance, and protection.

GOD WATCHERS TEACH DISCERNMENT

Discernment is not the same thing as self-righteous judgment. It has at least two parts.

Spiritual discernment is the ability to recognize the source of a spirit; to understand the source of circumstances and activity that cannot be determined with the five senses alone. Those trained in true Christ-centered discernment will sense the deep responsibility of seeing what few others can see. They respond to the Holy Spirit with holy knowledge as they peer into things that determine the life and death of everything in this dimension of time and space. Therefore, simply "seeing" what others do not see is not a sign of Christ-centered discernment. Seeing and reading another's spirit is far different from the Christ-centered discernment that gets to the heart of an issue with real solutions and hope. Just "reading someone's mail" accomplishes nothing and reveals immaturity. It is critical to test what you have seen and heard in the spirit realm. If the actions do not confirm the discernment, your response is to simply keep quiet until you have prayed the issue through. My experience is that many can read the spirit of the man without ever reading the Spirit of God.

There is a second function of discernment as well. Spiritual discernment is also evident as the "watchman on the wall" of a city. The watchman's job is to be aware of the surrounding countryside and the activity that is near him. The parent or parents in a family are primarily responsible to be the watchmen for the home. As the children grow older and are taught discernment themselves, they become prepared to watch their own lives. This also requires much prayer in order to be certain of what you are discerning.

True spiritual judgment is much like discernment but the immature will always run to the verse that we should not judge. Those who use this verse should not judge, for their lack of understanding moves them into the realm of fleshly accusations and turmoil in the name of spiritual judgment.

Becoming familiar with the feeling, the sense, the presence of His Spirit is the quickest way to develop a heart of discernment. When something right is going on, it feels right deep in your heart, deep in your soul.

But solid food is for the mature, who because of practice have their senses trained to discern good and evil (Hebrews 5:14).

LEARN FROM MY MISTAKES!

Back in the day, when heavy metal music came on the scene, it was customary for believers to bash this kind of music as demonic, rebellious, and just way too loud! Those were the days when I pastored a church. The young people there gave me a cassette tape of a Christian heavy metal band. Now to me, that was an oxymoron. There was no way a band could be both Christian and heavy metal. But as they talked, I felt a nudge in my spirit, so I refrained from condemning it without listening first.

I started playing it in my car and immediately thought there was something wrong with the stereo system. Then I quickly realized that there was nothing wrong at all, it was just the style of music that I did not like. But something amazing happened that day. As I listened, I immediately began to sense the flow of the Holy Spirit in what was apparently music coming out of the speakers. I had to laugh at myself. God was doing something that I did not care much for. I did not like the style and so condemned it as demonic. Wow, was I embarrassed. As I repented for my human reaction and condescending judgment, God spoke to me never to judge something spiritually that I already disliked naturally unless I am willing, deep in my heart, to have my mind changed.

Over the years, it has happened time and time again. I could hear our Lord Jesus's words to Saul on the road to Damascus when he was thrown from his horse:

He fell to the ground and heard a voice saying to him, "Saul, Saul, why are you persecuting Me?" (Acts 9:4)

JOB DESCRIPTION OF A GOD WATCHER

This then, is some of what a God watcher does. He sees what God is doing and distinguishes it from those who claim God is doing something completely different as related to His principles—the Word of God. Certainly, there are subjective factors when determining whether or not God is doing something specific, but the ways of God are open for little discussion. His mercy, for instance, will always rule the day. He always uses the broken, the humble, the hidden to do His work in the earth. These foundational building blocks of His life need to be laid in everyone's life. There is no bypassing these crucial elements of His life that are worked into our lives through suffering. They are not laid by words alone. These truths are encouraged by their consistent demonstration in the life of the one who teaches them. To have an intellectual understanding of truth without living it nullifies what is taught no matter how eloquently it is spoken. They are those who lay their heart on those they serve and not just their hands. Those who do not love have little lasting power in their words, their prayers, and their actions

The discernment of a God watcher is refined in the crucible of trials and hard times. He is able see beyond the spirit of a man to sense the Spirit of God in a situation. His discernment is pure, unjaded, uncompromised, and never politically, traditionally, monetarily, or religiously motivated. He sees from God's perspective, for God's purpose, in God's timing. He is not answerable to men, but painfully aware of his responsibility before God to speak only what he is sure he is seeing, nothing more and nothing less.

Chapter 9

BEHOLDING HIM IN SPIRIT AND IN WORD

GOD WATCHERS DO NOT RELY ON FORMULAS, SPIRITUAL REC-ipes, or someone else's experience. They are open before God to see what He wants in a particular situation. They know that they are not serving a franchised God. The Kingdom is not supposed to be like so many fast-food burger joints. God watchers don't aimlessly slap their hands on some-one and recite a few memorized phrases as though they are using incantation for their results. But then, that is why God watchers get results. They move out of a deep motivation of the Holy Spirit deep within and strength of discernment that makes them certain of what they say and do.

These men and women have seriously considered the fail-ure of our past and therefore they do not consider it heresy to rethink what they have believed for many years. They are not afraid of questions like, "If we are the light of the world, why are the nations not streaming to our light as Isaiah 60:3

declares?" Do we blame the world, the devil, or the light? Few consider self-examination of the beliefs we have gobbled up like a sparrow's blind hatchlings. These helpless peeps have their mouths open but their eyes closed, trusting whatever is dropped into their gullet.

SEARCH THE SCRIPTURES

You search the Scriptures because you think that in them you have eternal life; it is these that testify about Me; and you are unwilling to come to Me so that you may have life (John 5:39-40).

The open-hearted attitude of God watchers toward new ideas is often construed as an unwillingness to embrace foundational orthodoxy. But in reality, His life defines our understanding of our orthodoxy. To be sure, following our human experience has its place as it is renewed by Him, but it is the divine life that constantly redefines what we have always believed and unfolds the Word in the context of our very real experience.

I am often asked this question, "Which is higher, our experience or the Word of God?" But that is the wrong question. Only a fool would put experience ahead of the Word. But equally, only a fool would place the untested doctrine derived from the Word above our experience. When our experience differs from the Word, there is a conundrum. Sometimes what I believe is unscriptural. Sometimes what I am praying for is not God's timing. Sometimes what I believe is limiting what God really wants to do in my life. The bottom line is always the fruit of our faith. Fruit-proof is the final determination of the validity of what we do, what we believe. Fruit-proof is always recognizable with peace, courage, hope, and inner peace. While God's Word is absolute, what I believe about His Word is very much up for discussion. Of course, many can no longer distinguish the difference between their own personal doctrine and the Word, which is one reason the word *heretic* is thrown around so indiscriminately.

The second part of Jesus's statement is most telling, indeed. Jesus said, *"and you are unwilling to come to Me so that you may have life"* (John 5:40). It is far easier to interpret the Word apart from the Holy Spirit than it is to actually experience Jesus, the Living Word, in the context of His written Word. But now the proverbial cat is out of the bag. The written Word cannot be understood apart from the guidance of the Living Word, Jesus Christ. That is why it is imperative that I understand that much of what I believe, apart from the basic truths of salvation, is open for correction. I need the Holy Spirit. I need others, the Body of Christ, to be my balance.

Often God watchers are accused of extra-biblical belief. I have learned that the things most call *extra-biblical* are simply realities of God that many do not believe or have not experienced yet. Our lives in Him should be expanding. But we cannot grow if we are unwilling to be challenged in every part of our lives. I am not yet all I want to be, but I am yielding to Him more each day because I am responding to what I see in Him.

Growth demands the recognition of deeper understanding of the things that we have always embraced. But that does not nullify the uniqueness, validity, or truth of the

Bible. Rather, divine life as we interact with Him clarifies, corrects, and in some cases forces us to discard some things we believed that were just downright wrong. My pursuit of His reality demands my need to place the experience of the living God above the dogma of dry religious study. I do not fear what needs to change in my belief system, knowing that change is the precursor to a deeper interaction with my living Lord. My personal beliefs do not define me over the long term, as these change as my experience continues and the Living Word unites with the written Word in my heart. My relentless pursuit of Him is my defining element. I have come to see that what I have been taught may be the very thing that is keeping me from the very life I crave in my heart. I am discovering that my willingness to change is directly related to the passion I have to know Him in the power of His resurrection and, yes, in the fellowship of His suffering.

It would be a grave disservice to this book to say that I believe the reality of the written Word is dry and lifeless. Man's religion is dry and lifeless. It is boring, legalistic. It is finite and condemning. So many folks still follow these lifeless dogmas for fear of retaliation from those in control. It is for certain that those who see Him in all His glorious presence want to follow Him, obey Him, and allow Him to live His life through them. The fruit of seeing Him is becoming like Him. God's love, joy, peace, patience, gentleness, goodness, meekness, self-control, and faith will speak for themselves. Those who merely have an intellectual approach to God and are void of His presence will also be void of His ever-flowing life within.

CHANGED BY BEHOLDING HIM IN WORD AND SPIRIT

But we all, with unveiled face, beholding as in a mirror the glory of the Lord, are being transformed into the same image from glory to glory, just as from the Lord, the Spirit (2 Corinthians 3:18).

The more I see Him, the more I become like Him. Seeing Him as He truly is ignites a supernatural transformation that education alone cannot hope to accomplish. Seeing Him changes our spiritual DNA from self-centeredness to Christ-centeredness. This transformation is a continuous process of becoming a new person in Christ, of putting on His mind, living by His faith, and doing the works of His Father and mine. I begin to see as He sees, hear as He hears, and love as He loves. My motivation is no longer self-promotion. I am not looking for a "word" to impress anyone, nor do I write my own marketing plan as though I have a comedy routine or set of songs to sing and peddle from town to town. As I see, I do. If I do not see, I do nothing. I am becoming like Him—single-minded in love, restoration, and wholeness.

His glory cannot help but be seen in us as we see Him. But don't look for halos, gold dust, or feathers. The glory of God that changes the world is the glory of His life flowing out from you.

GOD IS SPIRITUALLY DISCERNED

My mind is not renewed by memorizing Scripture alone. We must yield to its truth and submit to the work of the Holy Spirit as He creates a habitation for His presence in our hearts. My mind is renewed by seeing Him wherever I am open to see Him. First in the Word, then in my prayer life, my daily routine, and my worship. *That* changes me from the inside. There is little that can withstand the exciting phenomenon of seeing Him as He is daily or even moment by moment. I am not waiting till I am "over there" to see Him. His Kingdom, His rule, and His reign is always intended for here, now, inside of us. Seeing Him now is most invigorating. He is changing me from what the world, the enemy, my past, and my personal prejudices have made me. Like a blooming flower, I become what He has always intended, now, in this life.

Yes, there is no doubt that seeing Him, living in His presence, is the key to everything we want to do, become, and experience. Of course, reading God's Word and meditating in His presence will always be a most necessary part of our lives, but that act in itself does not change us if we fail to see, spiritually speaking, the living Word in the written Word. We are changed when our minds are renewed. Our minds are renewed when we see Him. There is absolutely nothing like the transformational power of His presence. In His presence, there is no argument, no fight, no resistance. There is only bended knee at the wonder of His love, the beauty of His presence, the power of His truth.

On the other hand, I know so many "presence junkies" who have no discernment whatsoever. They just run after feelings and goose bumps all the time. The Word is critical as the plumb line of our spiritual experiences. As a God watcher, one of my favorite places to be is in the Scripture and I find rich communion with Him there. Jesus preached

Himself out of every book of the Old Testament to the men on the Emmaus road. His mind was *filled* with the Word. Granted, He understood it completely, but that is exactly why we need to study with His Spirit as the teacher. Nonetheless, these "presence junkies" do not discourage me from the reality of His manifest presence in my life.

A LIVING FAITH

The fact is, those who only know the Word intellectually stand out like a sore thumb against those who have encountered Him in it. Something wondrous happens when you realize you are in the presence of the King. There is a supernatural interaction between you and your Lord, which there are no words to describe. Just like a butterfly comes out of its cocoon and becomes something that it has no control over, the sons of God emerge in His presence as their spiritual DNA is released deep in their hearts. As much as some would want to think so, this supernatural transformation does not only happen in a Bible study but anywhere we are open to see Him at work.

God watchers discover that their faith must evolve from simply a philosophy to the dynamic relational experience it was intended to be. The intellectual aspect has validity, but only in the context of a living relationship. Otherwise, it is nothing more than studying old Latin, which is considered a dead language because it is no longer spoken. As a dead language, there is no further growth, expansion, or creativity with it, for it is life itself that adds the dynamic of growth. The nuances that come with a living language reflect the journey of the people who speak it. The foundational basis of the language never changes, but new words and new uses of old words are the natural outgrowth of life. A living language cannot remain static any more than a living cocoon can refuse to release the new beauty that is locked inside.

Please do not mistake "dead language" as though I am talking about the written Word of God. Once again, I am speaking of the dead lies of what many of us were told was real and was not. Those who will diligently search out the Word will find the richness of His reality and power of the living Spirit of God as they read. It is all you expect to see. If your heart is open, you will hear His Voice in every verse.

SURPRISED BY WHAT I SEE

I know I am seeing Him when I am surprised by what I see. It never gets old. I am shocked by what He shows me and it causes my spirit to leap within with an *"Amen!"* that shakes my soul. But too often, I am not opened to being shocked by Him. My brain dismisses these visions before I have a chance to consciously see them. I have to practice being open. I must *will* to see things I have never seen, hear things I have never heard. After all, that is the only way I will ever do things I have never done.

UTTERING THINGS UNLAWFUL TO SPEAK

Sometimes when I allow these "out of the box" moments to happen, I get brave enough to share them with someone only to discover that the resistance that I was able to avoid in myself is alive and well in others. I often wonder if God had already showed Himself to the person I was baring my heart too. They seem to have the denial so well prepared that

I am certain they used it before. So I think I am using a little more wisdom by being more careful who I share these times with. Although I have to be honest, the shock value of talking about these wondrous, unlawful things is entertaining. Nonetheless, I try to only share with those who understand, are searching, or need "shock therapy" in their walk with God. Paul had this experience and it changed him forever.

> *I knew a man in Christ above fourteen years ago, (whether in the body, I cannot tell; or whether out of the body, I cannot tell: God knoweth;) such an one caught up to the third heaven. And I knew such a man, (whether in the body, or out of the body, I cannot tell: God knoweth;) how that he was caught up into paradise, and heard unspeakable words, which it is not lawful for a man to utter* (2 Corinthians 12:2-4 KJV).

Paul saw things that were unlawful to speak. But unlawful according to whose opinion? Who was he referring to when he saw things that he couldn't repeat? Why would there be things that he saw in the third heaven that were against the law to utter? He could not repeat them according to the Law of Moses. According to the customs, traditions, and rituals of the day, he saw things that could get him in big trouble. Yet as we see, he talks about those things anyway. He saw things fulfilled in Christ that were still entrenched in Judaism. Peter experienced this same dilemma when he fell into a trance.

> *On the next day, as they were on their way and approaching the city, Peter went up on the housetop*

about the sixth hour to pray. But he became hungry and was desiring to eat; but while they were making preparations, he fell into a trance; and he saw the sky opened up, and an object like a great sheet coming down, lowered by four corners to the ground, and there were in it all kinds of four-footed animals and crawling creatures of the earth and birds of the air. A voice came to him, "Get up, Peter, kill and eat!" But Peter said, "By no means, Lord, for I have never eaten anything unholy and unclean." Again a voice came to him a second time, "What God has cleansed, no longer consider unholy" (Acts 10:9-15).

What Peter saw was unscriptural according to Judaism. It was unlawful to speak, let alone do. Nonetheless, you have to love Peter! He did both! He told everyone what happened and began to sit and eat with the Gentiles.

There is no doubt that God will show us things that are in direct opposition to what we have always believed, but they will not be in opposition to His Word, only perhaps our understanding of it. But there will be some like Peter and Paul who will not hesitate to speak out what they see Him doing. This has the effect of challenging those who do not see but it also has the effect of being marginalized by those who are certain of their theology. The irony is those who accuse you of error are often unwilling to see their own self-imposed limitations. But because they have the credentials of the religious system, they are able to successfully make the argument that it is you who are, in fact, rebellious and in error.

A disciple is not above his teacher, nor a slave above his master. It is enough for the disciple that he become like his teacher, and the slave like his master. If they have called the head of the house Beelzebul, how much more will they malign the members of his household! Therefore do not fear them, for there is nothing concealed that will not be revealed, or hidden that will not be known. What I tell you in the darkness, speak in the light; and what you hear whispered in your ear, proclaim upon the housetops. Do not fear those who kill the body but are unable to kill the soul; but rather fear Him who is able to destroy both soul and body in hell (Matthew 10:24-28).

My passion to know Him compels me to search the Scriptures, to see Him with all the clarity that His mercy and my personal limitations permit. My direction is *forward*. I fear Him more than I fear a man. I know I am naked before Him. I know He sees me, hears me, watches me, and is more attentive to me than I can possibly imagine. For that reason I walk softly, circumspectly carrying in my heart the weighty responsibility of my words. My allegiance is to Him. For this I get the credit or the blame for what I see in Him. I accept that responsibility as mine and mine alone. Anything less does not give me the right to say the things I say.

ONENESS

Our oneness with Him precedes our unity with o' For when we experience Jesus on a regular, tangib presence transcends disagreements that divide and doctrinal issues that build walls around certain camps of belief. The true nature of God gathers us—not into one building, one denomination, but into one Spirit. The greatness of God lifts our hearts to see Him in Spirit. Once a person begins to experience this other-worldly reality, the things that divide us seem so absurd, and absurd they are! We will never comprehend with a finite mind all that our infinite Lord really is. How can we really believe we have Him figured out? The intellect will lead us astray because our intellect is incapable of understanding the things of the Spirit.

It is not that doctrine is not important, it is just that doctrine shouldn't be what divides us. In fact, there is nothing that should divide us. I am learning how to refocus my thinking when I am with those who believe differently. In my heart, I know that as we all see Him more clearly, our agreement will increase. In the meantime, our unity is in our mutual faith, accepting that we all see in part. We should all continually assume that there are areas within us that need adjustment and greater light. It could even be that my part is the one that needs to be adjusted.

Chapter 10

THE GOOD, THE BAD, THE REALITY

Where your treasure is, there your heart will be also. The eye is the lamp of the body; so then if your eye is clear, your whole body will be full of light. But if your eye is bad, your whole body will be full of darkness. If then the light that is in you is darkness, how great is the darkness! (MATTHEW 6:21-23)

YOU KNOW WHO YOU ARE. YOU HAVE QUESTIONED YOURSELF for years. Tested your heart. Studied and restudied the Word. You wondered why you could not be satisfied the way so many others are satisfied; why you could not be content with what you have heard from the pulpit and from some "leaders," as it was so different from what you were hearing deep within your spirit. Yes, I know you better than you think. You have this burning, this dissatisfaction with things as they are, and you are unwilling to accept them as the way things ought to be. You know better. You have allowed Brokenness to touch your life. You have allowed her to teach you what no man-led Bible study based on the traditions of men and no seminary could ever dream of teaching. You are not alone! You carry in your heart, in your soul, the mark, the brand of Him with whom you have made covenant, and there is nothing that will ever satisfy you apart from union with your Creator King.

Few understand the work of God in God watchers. Fewer, perhaps, believe that God has been able to do anything in them. But that is only because these folks see their Lord, their world, through eyes that have not peered into the unseen realm. Their point of reference is the system of redundant religion. There is no possible way for those who have never explored the realm of Spirit, or at least hungered for more of that experience, to have a clue as to what makes God watchers tick. Of course, sometimes it is not so cut and dried. Often, folks just didn't "see" some of the things that you have seen. In any case, you must make it a point to resist any voice that would encourage you to harbor a holier-than-thou attitude against them. It is crucial that you hold them with honor and recognize all that is *good* in them and their ministry.

If we do not watch our hearts, we risk skewing our vision and our own walk with Jesus. Remember that God watchers, like everyone else, see "in part."

To those around you, you may seem to be the oddball, the loner, the renegade, the troublemaker, problem child, accuser-of-the-brethren. In their eyes, you may appear to be unsettled, unsure, emotionally out of control, shallow, and unteachable because you refuse to bow to their paradigms. But they cannot perceive what God has wrought in your soul. They have no idea of the work of the Spirit deep within. Nonetheless, our response to their, shall we say, less then complementary attitudes confirms the life of our precious Lord within. Our response to this attitude will show the level of maturity that has been achieved in our hearts. You must never confuse passion with maturity, for they are vastly different, indeed. The young in Christ are often open to see marvelous things in God, but their immaturity often causes others to reject not only them but the things they have seen. But Brokenness is a faithful companion. If you are willing, what you see in Christ will become etched in your heart through allowing the suffering we all experience to work for our good, our maturity.

The real test for God watchers is not to allow those who judge them to disturb their peace, their inner well-being. The worst thing one can do is lash out at the uninformed, the inexperienced, thus proving their point. In other words, your actions can justify their negative assessment of the God watcher. For if you really have seen Him, you are undoubtedly becoming like Him, drenched in His love, overflowing with the fruit of the Spirit, and unsinkable by the most vile attack. Your life is growing in love, mercy, and compassion.

There is a reason Jesus instructed us to pray for our enemies or those we perceive to be against us. There is nothing more compelling than praying for these folks. God will soften your heart and help you to see from their perspective. This will most certainly give you peace and release you from your own negative attitudes that can prevent you from moving on in maturity.

The deep calling of the Lord in our hearts is not a frivolous event. It is a solemn reality of an eternal God gathering His children to Himself. Those who answer and begin allowing Him to live through them will display His love, His mercy, and His power indiscriminately, at least in our human view, to those God leads us to, even our "enemies" and those who oppose us. Our obedient response without hesitation, argument, or rebuttal will change lives for eternity. But this is the true adventure, the real excitement of the journey with Him. This is the abundant life, knowing that you are making a difference in spite of what others say or do to you.

GOD WATCHERS LAY DOWN THEIR WILL TO HIS WILL…EVEN WHEN IT HURTS

The notion that those who follow Jesus have an almost idyllic life is seriously flawed. The people who believe that everything should come easily are not following Jesus, but a fabricated religious worldview that demands life should be a breeze because Jesus is taking care of everything.

God watchers see the Father as He is moving in the same Spirit as Jesus did when He walked the earth. We may not find ourselves raising the dead (although we may), but we will certainly find ourselves in amazing situations because we do what we see Him doing. Remember, Jesus was a walking miracle. But He was also a walking target for the system of religion that did not want Him to disturb the established order of the day. The life of Jesus was powerful, but tiring; extravagant, but lonely; engaging, but dangerous; fulfilling, but disconcerting. Listening to His apostles by reading the Gospels, you come to see this description is accurate. There is absolutely no way around the simple reality that all of Jesus's true disciples will experience what He experienced, for the disciple is not above his master.

> Remember the word that I said to you, "A slave is not greater than his master." If they persecuted Me, they will also persecute you; if they kept My word, they will keep yours also. But all these things they will do to you for My name's sake, because they do not know the One who sent Me (John 15:20-21).

That is why being a God watcher is scary business to the pride we battle with. Seeing what God is doing and then doing the same thing in time and space may look and sound exciting, but at the end of the day, it leads to the cross, to death to self, loss of reputation, friends, careers, and eventually could even lead to physical death. There is no way to skirt the issue; to be a God watcher takes us to the same end that Jesus experienced. Sure, He experienced the glory of resurrection, but not before the shame of suffering and crucifixion.

Truly, being a God watcher will bring on persecution from everywhere, even from those whom you counted as friends. It brings dying daily to a new reality and can eventually lead to physical death for the sake of the Gospel. Becoming a genuine God watcher is where the separation of the sheep and the goats really comes in. Few will give their lives for something they are not sure of. Few will risk persecution for a personal kingdom, a private interpretation of a Bible verse, or a Lord they do not really know.

Loving Him is the joy of a God watcher's life. Loving Him unto death is the ultimate act of worship.

> *For this reason the Father loves Me, because I lay down My life so that I may take it again. No one has taken it away from Me, but I lay it down on My own initiative. I have authority to lay it down, and I have authority to take it up again. This commandment I received from My Father* (John 10:17-18).

Trials, then, are recognized not as the horrible activity of satan, but as they really are—the continuous love of God, who is determined to have His way in those who have invited Him to change them. How many times do we resist the will of God by fighting circumstances so vehemently that we cannot bear to see what God is doing in our hearts. We believers have such a preoccupation with the good life that we forget that trials do such a deep work within that it cannot be measured. Brokenness contends with us so that we can ultimately live the life we were always intended to live.

THE REST OF THE GOD WATCHER

It is probably impossible to be a God watcher and be focused on ourselves. Self-focus guarantees that we will forfeit the opportunity to be a God watcher and hence a doer of the word instead of just seeing it. Self-focus shows itself in many ways.

For instance, when we concentrate on how we can get to God instead of realizing that we are *in* Him and He is *in* us, the focus is all about us. The mistake is a classic self-centered ploy. Faith that is based on my needs, wants, and wanton desires is a form of religion that makes us think we are in God's will just because He is taking care of us.

For instance, many are led to believe that God is there simply to make our lives easier. While it is true that those who belong to Jesus will recognize a great degree of the miraculous, that is not necessarily why He came. God watchers are not watching to see and understand how they can "get more" from Him. They watch so they can more completely yield to Him.

He has and is and always will take care of me. Our human nature is to focus on the care, safety, and provision for ourselves and our families. But God takes care of us because we are Him. Jesus said:

> But seek first His kingdom and His righteousness, and all these things will be added to you. So do not worry about tomorrow; for tomorrow will care for itself. Each day has enough trouble of its own (Matthew 6:33-34).

Jesus showed us what is important. He takes care of us so we can seek Him and His Kingdom.

> Ask, and it will be given to you; seek, and you will find; knock, and it will be opened to you. For everyone who asks receives, and he who seeks finds, and to him who knocks it will be opened (Mathew 7:7-8).

> Look at the birds of the air, that they do not sow, nor reap nor gather into barns, and yet your heavenly

Father feeds them. Are you not worth much more than they? And who of you by being worried can add a single hour to his life? And why are you worried about clothing? Observe how the lilies of the field grow; they do not toil nor do they spin, yet I say to you that not even Solomon in all his glory clothed himself like one of these. But if God so clothes the grass of the field, which is alive today and tomorrow is thrown into the furnace, will He not much more clothe you? You of little faith! (Mathew 6:26-30)

We God watchers are bearers of good news. The more we see Him, the more good news we have and the more joy we have to deliver it with. Seeing Him shows us His heart, not only for others but for ourselves as well. There is precious little to complain about when we have seen who He is and what He has for us. Seeing Him also causes us to worry less and less about ourselves and even what others think of us. The discovery of His total care for us is quite unbelievable. We really are in the palm of His hands.

Everything that concerns us personally concerns Him, no matter who we are, what we have done, or how we think we have failed Him. This is not a license to live a licentious lifestyle; it is a license to understand that He forgives and removes guilt. He takes care of our weakness so we can fulfill our reason to live.

The clearer we see Him, the more we find ourselves giving ourselves to Him instead of to the lusts of the flesh and the crazy things we are tempted with. Our hearts are stayed on Him. Our hunger to know and experience Him increases as we interact with Him. He overtakes our thoughts, desires, and actions. We find ourselves yielding in ways we never thought possible. Troubling sins and weaknesses that always seemed to haunt us seem to have less and less control over us. We are becoming like Him. Or rather, we are allowing Him to live His life through us.

God watchers have abandoned themselves to the work of the Cross, fearing neither those who presumptuously try to take control of the church Jesus is building nor the intimidation that pours from their mouths. They are ones of whom the world is not worthy. They are the poor, the broken, the forgotten of men, but filled with the fire of God. Their lives flow with God's love and mercy. They are branded with the eternal seal of brokenness. Their lips pour forth honey and milk. Their hearts ache for His presence. They die daily, allowing His life to flow through them to a world in desperate need.

They speak hope, justice, love, healing, wholeness, and peace. They are true gatherers. They labor with their Lord while leaving judgment to the Judge, and instead call together all who will be gathered unto Him. They see Him high and lifted above all principalities and powers. The work is finished. The final words of Jesus echo with exhilaration and finality in their spirits and throughout all time. What they see defines who they are and what they see unveils Scripture in a way that mere intellectual assent cannot begin to understand.

God watchers know that they have the best news that anyone could ever hope to deliver to another human being. Sometimes we think the good news is *judge into repentance*, but that is not our ministry. There is one judge and lawgiver and He is not a man, thank God.

> *There is only one Lawgiver and Judge, the One who is able to save and to destroy; but who are you who judge your neighbor?* (James 4:12)

Personally, I still do not understand why folks would not want to see Him as He is, full of love and desire, overflowing with resolve to redeem the world and with the intention to love each one of us with His divine love and favor.

TRANSFORMED FROM THE INSIDE

There are few things left to argue about and fewer things to fear when we see Him as He is. He has everything under control. As Jesus prayed, His Kingdom is coming; His will is being done in the hearts of those who are open to Him. The daily anticipation and moment-by-moment experience of His will and work in our life is the joy that gives us strength and peace. In spite of our occasional rebellion, sin, and unbelief, He knows our hearts. He is undeterred by the things that cause us to worry and fret. Living in an attitude of "yes" toward God changes the dynamic of how we pray and what we perceive as His attitude toward us. This attitude of *unconditional* is quite a paradox. Surrendering to Him releases us into a freedom that cannot adequately be explained. His presence fills the mind, the soul, and the body.

The process of submitting our will to His will becomes an anticipation of greater joy and deeper union with Him. We discover that dying daily can be something we look forward to with understanding, by experience that His ways are not just higher than our ways, they are a heck of a lot more meaningful, fruitful, and yes, a lot more fun.

We are discovering that He has the ability to heal in less than a blink of an eye. But there is something bigger than that at work in the hearts of those who love Him and who know He is building Himself within. Because we are discovering the completeness, the finality of His work on the Cross for our salvation, it is clear that He is doing what is best for us. My attitude is simple—I am in His hands. So even more than receiving healing, I want to be conformed into His image. More than all my perceived needs being met, I want such total union with Him that people do not see me, they see Him alone. With ecstatic assurance I can shout it from the housetops:

> *…it is no longer I who live, but Christ lives in me; and the life which I now live in the flesh I live by faith in the Son of God, who loved me and gave Himself up for me* (Galatians 2:20).

I have nothing to protect, no one to convince, no one to appease. I am an open book. I am just me. But with Him shining His life through me, I speak as I see. I am a God watcher. That is what I do. Everything else is up to Him. He is within, changing me as I see Him. This is not an issue of pride. It is an issue of focused anticipation and joy. He is dynamically at work, and His work is predictable and constant. I am forever on the Potter's wheel. I can forever feel His loving hands molding, shaping, forming me into a vessel that adequately contains His essence and displays His life most accurately.

So then, this is how we are called to live—abundantly, joyfully, while living out all God has dreamed for us. Yes, there is no question that being a God watcher is a way of life like none other.

Chapter 11

WATCHMEN! HOW GOES THE NIGHT?

One keeps calling to me from Seir, "Watchman, how far gone is the night?" (ISAIAH 21:11)

GOD WATCHERS SEE INTO THE "NIGHT," THE REALM OF SPIRIT that cannot be reached by our five senses. These folks see what others cannot see. They are not a select group, as all those who seek Him can see into the night, into the spirit. As they look, they see things incredible but terrible, awesome but terrifying, true but challenging. Would to God that His people will rise to the challenge of seeing Him with the courage, the resolve necessary to accurately proclaim and do just what they are seeing. If God watchers do not come forth, the church and world will be left to the blindness of those who cannot see beyond time and space to where the genuine

147

solutions to the world's problems await the proclamation that will release their power into time and space.

> *Arise, shine; for your light has come, and the glory of the Lord has risen upon you. For behold, darkness will cover the earth and deep darkness the peoples; but the Lord will rise upon you and His glory will appear upon you. Nations will come to your light, and kings to the brightness of your rising* (Isaiah 60:1-3).

God watchers are not interested in their own agenda. In fact, true God watchers have no agenda. They are impassioned with only one thing. They want to see what He is doing and proclaim it and participate in what they see. These are folks who have traveled far with Brokenness. They have sat at her feet and have learned, through the things they have suffered, that the only worthwhile endeavor is co-laboring with the One they have given up all to serve.

They see the world from an eternal perspective. They see God and His workings in the earth as the carefully orchestrated plan that is being fulfilled at exactly the right times and seasons. Therefore, momentary light affliction does not distract or detour them. They know they are a part of something much bigger than themselves. They understand that the torch they carry is a temporary honor to be passed on as their generation is called home. They carry within themselves the dying of Christ, so that He might shine more fully through them.

You will recognize them as those who always seem to have time for the needy, a prayer for the broken, a word of encouragement to one who cannot make it through the day. They will embrace the unlovable, knowing they themselves can also appear less than attractive to the well-adjusted. Because they watch God, they know His compassion and so allow it to flow through them. They have tasted of His love and so let that love flow freely through them. They are ones you want to be with when you are in need. You already know that for these folks, serving is not a burden, it is why they breathe. They will pray for you or take you shopping when your car is being repaired; comfort you or help you clean the house; teach you the Scriptures or bring dinner when you are sick. True God watchers can be recognized a mile away.

> *Truly I say to you, to the extent that you did it to one of these brothers of Mine, even the least of them, you did it to Me* (Matthew 25:40).

> *So faith comes from hearing, and hearing by the word of Christ. But I say, surely they have never heard, have they? Indeed they have; "Their voice has gone out into all the earth, and their words to the ends of the world"* (Romans 10:17-18).

"Silence! I kill you!"
—*Achmed, the Dead Terrorist* by Jeff Dunham

We must remember that the goal of fleshly men, religion, and the enemy is to silence the God watcher. The Word must become flesh, but the Word must first be heard before it is spoken and then it must be spoken in faith. If the Word can be stopped before it is even spoken, it is easy for the system to win. That is I why I hammer away at this topic so often. The resistance to God from everywhere is relentless. We must be free and secure in Him to allow what we see in our hearts to flow freely from our mouths as well as our lives. The onslaught of the opposition is often successful in silencing us. But the result of their intimidation is so diabolical! We don't usually stop talking because of their threats; we just start saying what has already been said, thus removing the threat of saying what will tear down the works of the enemy.

When I only say what has already been seen, and say what has already been said, I am not a God watcher, but merely a spokesman for the status quo. The dusty words spoken by those who are afraid to declare what they really see is one reason our faith appears to be just like old Latin—dead. It is a laughingstock to the world and an embarrassment to our children. My brethren, this ought not to be so! But is so because folks like us allow ourselves to be marginalized and silenced by those who do not want to see change. When we allow ourselves to be silenced, we stunt spiritual growth and true Christlikeness. We will never see it emerge on this planet.

It is easy to criticize the world's systems and the religious for their moral and spiritual bankruptcy until it is understood that the silence of the believer has allowed pervasive attitudes to go unchecked. We should be as passionate about the *now* as an angry she-bear seeing her little cubs in peril. In a reality, our "cubs" *are* in peril. God has chosen to do His bidding through the likes of simple folks like you and me. If we wait for leaders to do something, we are already destroyed. The church system has been saying the same things, doing the same things for centuries, yet the world continues on the path of annihilation. If the things we said and believed worked, the fruit-proof of our faith would be visible. It is the time for seasoned men and women of God to rise to the occasion and begin to watch God, see what He is doing, and offer themselves as a living sacrifice so He can do His will through them.

DEAD RELIGION VERSUS LIVING GOD

As I have said throughout this book, it is not the ingenuity of man that reveals God's glory to the earth. It is not man's massive organizations that bring peace and hope to humanity. The activity of God is proceeding as it always has—from Spirit, in Spirit to a thirsty world. The will of God is done where it has always been done—in the hearts of those who respond to Him on earth and as a matter of course in heaven. The silence of the heavens is only among those who are not listening. But more importantly, the apparent silence of God is buffeted by those who do not want a living God, One who is concerned with His creation.

But for you and me, let us allow Him full and unhindered access to us and to those we touch every day. This, then, is where our obedience counts. Be obedient to the flow of the River within, knowing that the same River that heals, restores, gathers, and forgives others through you is the same River that cleanses and changes you as He flows through you to others.

GOD'S PASSION

The reality and determination of the Father to truly fellowship with us is far too great for me to put into words. The mighty River of God's presence is flowing in us. Too many have been taught to wait for God, wait for the River. I understand that there needs to be the assurance that it is truly the River of His presence, but here is the sober truth. We are not waiting for the River. The River is waiting for us. He is the River and it flows through us. We cannot jump into something that we have become. My heart is now like a fire that is being blown upon by a Wind that is constant, powerful, purposeful, and never-ending.

The journey of a God watcher will not be an easy one, but it is exciting and fulfilling. It will not be a popular one, but He is the difference that keeps God watchers going forward full steam. I dare say, it will sometimes feel as though it is not worth the fight. But the growing reality of His ever-present Spirit will urge you on. The millions whom God has prepared are waiting. They will hear and they will respond to you as you carefully unveil what you have seen.

> *Get yourself up on a high mountain, O Zion, bearer of good news, lift up your voice mightily, O Jerusalem, bearer of good news; lift it up, do not fear. Say to the cities of Judah, "Here is your God!"* (Isaiah 40:9)

In spite of those who will always try to discourage you, there are countless millions of desperate folks who are starving to see the Lord for who He really is and want to know Him as you are coming to know Him and experience Him. There are plenty who will listen to you. You need to just start talking about who you see. More and more folks will want to know how you do it. If what you are saying is real, it will resonate. Folks will soon begin to respond to Him. But if you want to get them responding to you or just get them into your church, you will have to try way harder. Folks don't usually follow dust. They may not have experienced much of His love, but they are not stupid either.

SPIRITUAL DISCOVERIES

A lion has roared! Who will not fear? The Lord God has spoken! Who can but prophesy? (Amos 3:8)

I have discovered things that could get me hanged. Hum, they still might, come to think about it. We have developed doctrines to explain our lack, our loss, our sporadic times of victory, and the apparent erratic nature of His presence. We make seeking Him hard and finding Him harder. We put conditions on prayer and list mountains of reasons why we don't get what we want, as though God is running a spiritual butler service or worse, a "Believer's Got Doctrine" with the winner getting everything they ask for. Of course, that is the point. No one ever wins because no one ever does anything right.

We explain the elusive nature of revival by saying God was done "moving" or by blaming the folks for not being hungry anymore. We invent doctrine to explain away the things we don't experience, all while the people of God starve for a cool drink of spiritual water and the affirming word that would release them to pursue what is awaiting them in God's plan. God is calling folks like you and me to carry the good news of His boundless love, the endless possibilities and the focused determination of our Lord toward humanity. Look within, where He dwells, and allow Him to live through you.

Our Father has done everything to make it simple. Walking with Him is not always easy, but neither is it complicated. We are forgiven, once and for all; we are filled, once and for all; we are called, equipped, favored, and sent. He has done everything so we can joyfully carry the life of Jesus to the nations of the world. If we think that what we have been preaching is good news, just wait until the emergence of those who really know they are forgiven and discover the *really* Good News from the throne of God within. The world is in for the emergence of God's manifestation, the likes of which has never before been imagined, as average folks like you and me know for certain that we are forgiven, forgiven, and forgiven. Folks who actually believe the depth of His love and respond to it.

Yes, you have plenty to say. You have seen more than most. Your validation is that He has put His Spirit within you and is opening the heavens to show things that are unlawful to utter, things into which angels long to look. Certainly there will be opposition as there is when a plow is dropped in the ground after years of being fallow. Certainly there are folks waiting for His Spirit to sink deeply into their pain, their uncertainty, their hope, their faith. It will bring healing in the deepest part of who they are.

> *Who is this coming up from the wilderness, leaning*
> *on her beloved?* (Song of Solomon 8:5)

The answer to that question is simple. It is you. Leaning on you, Lord. Broken, submitted, meek, gentle, and roaring like the lion of Judah.

Chapter 12

RISE OF THE GOD WATCHERS

Come, let us return to the Lord. For He has
torn us, but He will heal us; He has wounded
us, but He will bandage us. He will revive us
after two days; He will raise us up on the third
day, that we may live before Him. So let us
know, let us press on to know the Lord. His
going forth is as certain as the dawn; and He
will come to us like the rain, like the spring
rain watering the earth (HOSEA 6:1-3).

WE ARE NOW PAYING THE PRICE OF A BOGUS RELIGIOUS SYS-
tem that has miserably failed humanity. The leadership in
governments, art, the media, entertainment, education, and
the courts are the product of this religious system that so
many are blindly and desperately clinging to. This generation

of opinion makers struggled through their early years suffering the pain, disappointment, and genuine heartache of a failed system that used and abused them in many ways. Many of these folks had religious backgrounds or were, in a significant way, affected by religion. I have talked to enough of them to know that what many are doing, now that they have an audience and therefore authority, is in direct response to what they experienced. It is payback for all the years of their own suffering.

What we are seeing now is the purposeful disregard of our values and the open opposition to our faith. These are a direct result of the utter failure of religion to deliver even a fraction of what it touted as its divine purpose and calling. I am not talking about the church Jesus is building, but I am referring to the backlash of yesterday's youth group members, altar boys, Sunday school attendees. When what is taught at these services is not seen in the lives of those who teach, disenchantment is the result and there is no one to blame but ourselves. Had we fulfilled our godly roles years ago, the secularized media, school system, and government would have had no audience to begin with.

But do not worry! His life will increase substantially, consistently, and beautifully as we learn to decrease. Don't be discouraged into silence. You are essential for His plan as all are who respond to Him. As long as there are those who will not be afraid to see Him and submit to His life within them, the flame of God's love shines triumphantly on the earth.

Then He said to me, "It is done. I am the Alpha and the Omega, the beginning and the end. I will give to the one who thirsts from the spring of the water of life without cost. He who overcomes will inherit these things, and I will be his God and he will be My son" (Revelation 21:6-7).

His promise is more than casual words dropped to us by an acquaintance. They are words filled with desire, longing, hopeful anticipation that there will be some who will begin to understand, at least in a small way, that His purpose will be done and that He has determined to fulfill that purpose through the likes of simple folks like you and me, who, having come to Him, love Him; having heard Him, want to please Him; and having experienced His presence, have become addicted to His nearness and have fallen hopelessly in love with Him. Having seen Him, we can recognize the wonder of His love and certainty of His determination to bring us into all He wants us to be.

IF I AM LIFTED UP

This then, is the time of His rising. But He will not—to be sure, *cannot*—arise alone. For He has purposed to be seen, to be revealed to the world through His Body, of which you and I are a part. Jesus said:

Now judgment is upon this world; now the ruler of this world will be cast out. And I, if I am lifted up from the earth, will draw all men to Myself (John 12:31-32).

We all love to lift Him up in worship and praise, but Jesus speaks of a more recognizable form of lifting Him up. When

Jesus is Lord in our lives, He becomes our Head, whom all can see. The head cannot be seen when the body is lying down, sitting down, or cast down under the burden of circumstances. But Jesus told us that when the Body stands up, the Head of the Body is automatically raised up high for all to see.

But there is a price to pay for this. To be part of the Body of our Lord Jesus Christ means that, among many other things, we will be looked upon as examples of life and faith. We are expressing the very life of Jesus. This is not taken lightly by our Lord. Brokenness is the key to carry such divinity and express such eternal love. Broken folks yield to Him in grateful worship and are continually offering themselves as living sacrifices so He can shine more completely through the likes of us.

Consider how men have abused the power of government and suppressed and committed such horrible atrocities upon their fellow human beings. I cannot image the mayhem that would ensue if divine power and authority were suddenly dropped on unbroken believers. There is no doubt—to run from the work of Brokenness is to stall the work of yielded transformation in our lives. Therefore, seeing the Body of Christ arise will be a testimony of His love and resurrection power in, to, and through humanity. This is the Christ of God whom the world is waiting to see. This is the light of the world. This is the city on a hill. This is the gathering heart, the compassionate heart, the loving heart of God expressed though simple folks like you and me.

I am not ashamed of who I am or where I started. I am not ashamed of the path I have struggled through. I am not ashamed to be hidden. I am His. I am shining. I am who I *am* by the grace of God. Men of importance may not see me, but the Man sees me and is pleased. This is my rest; my hope my *now*. God's people are manifesting His life as we speak. You are manifesting His life as you read these simple words. Yield, respond, give, pour out your heart to Him, to others, and you will show His glory now, through yourself. You will no longer run to a meeting to see pixie dust, feathers, or gold teeth. You *are* the meeting place of God and man in this life, right now. Behold, He comes!

For those who can hear Him, He is most definitely speaking—*Come to Me, all you who are working your fingers to the bone in an effort to please Me.* Jesus said:

> *Come to Me, all who are weary and heavy-laden, and I will give you rest. Take My yoke upon you and learn from Me, for I am gentle and humble in heart, and you will find rest for your souls. For My yoke is easy and My burden is light* (Matthew 11:28-30).

To serve Him, to do His bidding is joyful, peaceful, certain, and fulfilling. Each day begins with a sense of anticipation with the knowledge that His mercies are new with each new sunrise. With the rising of the sun is the real prospect that you are at His service and that what you do, say, feel, and pray has eternal consequences. For you are not like most who are confined to time and space. You are not limited in the way of those who do not see or do not care to see beyond their five senses.

THE CITY ON A HILL

The world changes when Jesus comes on the scene. The world changes when His will is done—when His love, compassion, power, and His life flow as freely through His Body now as it flowed through Him 2,000 years ago. When, without pretense or personal agenda, He shines through us with only His will at heart, the world runs to His light, just like a city set up on a hill. In the final analysis, it is only a change of heart that changes the world permanently.

Nowhere on earth is this more aptly demonstrated than in the Italian countryside. The villages and hamlets in Italy were built high on hills and mountains a thousand years ago to add more protection from bands of robbers and marauders. Today, the picturesque towns are still occupied, but with a big difference. Lights illumine the streets and lead up the winding roads to the homes and businesses along the way. They can be seen from miles away. As one travels on the highways after dark, every lighted mountaintop is a constant reminder of the Light of the world, the candle that should be not wasted under a bushel, and the city set on a hill. Micah's prophetic proclamation shouts with crisp confirmation of this when he declares.

> *And it will come about in the last days that the mountain of the house of the Lord will be established as the chief of the mountains. It will be raised above the hills, and the peoples will stream to it. Many nations will come and say, "Come and let us go up to the mountain of the Lord..."* (Micah 4:1-2).

When the light of the glory of God shines *through* us, rather than merely to us or on us, the world sees Him; the world changes. Our mountains of religious activity have not accomplished what will be done in a moment of time through those who yield in humble brokenness to Him. We are the lamp of His presence, His glory. We should not have to point to His glory or go to a special meeting to see it. It is true; we are His glory.

The children of Israel were so different from all the other nations and their gods because of one very clear distinction—Israel's God was with them. Israel's God was manifest. He was visible among them. The nations feared Israel because they feared their God, who watched over His people with the fierce jealousy of a mother protecting her little children. No wonder the Scriptures recount so often that the nations trembled at the mention of the name of Israel.

Isaiah prophesied the coming of the Messiah and announced His name, "Immanuel"—*God with us* (see Isa. 7:14). He has always been *with* His people. But, as it was in ancient Israel, His presence only benefits us when we allow Him to go before us, to be the lamp to our feet, the light to our path. When Israel went into war without the Lord going before them, their defeat was certain. Their advantage—rather, their victory—was that God was with them, went before them and fought their battles for them.

Today, no one seems to know where God is. Few understand that God is with the believer. Truth is, not many believers know that for a certainty. If we are not sure that God is with us, that He will go before us, how will anyone else know it? Many talk like God is with them but live like everyone else—full of fear and uncertainty. Many believers see God as in heaven but not in them. In fact, the very foundation of developing into a mature God watcher is to see Him and fellowship with Him within. But Jesus said, *"...lo, I am with you always, even to the end of the age"* (Matt. 28:20).

Jesus gave the assurance that His plan had always been to indwell His people. We can rest in His promise, knowing that He is within. Jesus also said:

> I will ask the Father, and He will give you another
> Helper, that He may be with you forever; that is
> the Spirit of truth, whom the world cannot receive,
> because it does not see Him or know Him, but you
> know Him because He abides with you and will be
> in you. I will not leave you as orphans; I will come
> to you. After a little while the world will no longer
> see Me, but you will see Me; because I live, you will
> live also. In that day you will know that I am in
> My Father, and you in Me, and I in you (John
> 14:16-20).

It is difficult to understand at first, but as I said earlier, simply acting like Jesus, talking like Jesus, or even trying to live like Jesus is not the answer. The world changes when Jesus can show Himself to the world through us. The world needs to see Him for who He truly is, not us acting like Him.

If we could do this all on our own, there would not have been a reason for Him to come. So, just as the Lord dwelled with ancient Israel, He dwells with us and in us. As ancient Israel allowed God to go before them in battle to ensure victory, so He will bring us to victory every time we allow

Him to have His way in us, around us, and through us. Our lessons from ancient Israel are many, but some of the more important include humility, softness of heart, and brokenness. These three lessons keep us in a position to see what the Lord is doing and allow Him to do His mighty work through you and me.

God has a one-track mind. He will bring us forth in maturity, in the full and perfect image of His Son. He is fashioning us to be those through whom all the world will be blessed. But God has always been single-minded toward His plan for humanity. When the people of Israel were discouraged after they were freed from Egypt and found themselves in the wilderness, Moses encouraged them with these words:

> *"He brought us out from there* [Egypt] *in order to bring us* in [to the Promised Land], *to give us the land which He had sworn to our fathers." So the Lord commanded us to observe all these statutes, to fear the Lord our God for our good always and for our survival, as it is today* (Deuteronomy 6:23-24).

THE ROLE OF BROKENNESS
IN THE LIFE OF A SON

I know this is always a recurring theme. My goal is to allow Him to do whatever He needs to do in order to bring me to a close friendship with Brokenness. Ah, but maybe some of you are a bit like me. I thought I could be the poster child for a broken and a contrite heart. I figured that Brokenness and I were buds; we understood each other, she knew I could always be counted on. The most painful discovery was when

I came to understand that I was not all that. Brokenness brought me to circumstances I could not handle, temptations that I could not resist. I found myself floundering for forgiveness and crying out for the strength that I discovered I did not have and for the mercy that I was not so willing to show to others.

Ah, yes, Brokenness—love her or hate her, she will bring us to exactly where we need to be in order to be a willing vessel for His glory. It is a lifetime process, which, in itself, is a confession born out experience with Brokenness.

I have learned, painfully discovered that my search should never be for the things He provides. For instance, I am not searching for healing. I do not want a formula to gain finances. I am not looking for a way, a method to entice folks to follow Him. He can do all that and more if I simply allow Him to be Himself, as He is, in me and through me. When my goal is simply to yield to Him who dwells within, everything I want to happen will happen in its own time and according to the will and purpose of our Lord. Therefore I can always remain at rest, at peace with the knowledge that He holds the reins of my life. He flows freely through me and does His work. Although He is using me, I often look at what He is doing through me as a bystander. I am hearing His words on my lips, sensing His love in my heart and His mercy toward the ones I am with. I become aware that I am merely a vessel of clay holding the glory of God.

Because He lives inside of me, I can do everything. *"I can do all things through Him who strengthens me"* (Phil. 4:13). I no longer serve Him with a gift I used to hang on to as assurance that He has truly called me. Everything He is now dwells inside of me—and all who call upon Him! In one sense, we are all parts of His Body, but that sacred truth does not limit what I can do. When the need arises, I do whatever needs to be done. Whatever I see Him doing, I have the confidence that He will move through me. So, with heart of yielded brokenness, I let Him do what He wants through me.

> *For this reason I bow my knees before the Father, from whom every family in heaven and on earth derives its name, that He would grant you, according to the riches of His glory, to be strengthened with power through His Spirit in the inner man; so that Christ may dwell in your hearts through faith; and that you, being rooted and grounded in love, may be able to comprehend with all the saints what is the breadth and length and height and depth, and to know the love of Christ which surpasses knowledge, that you may be filled up to all the fullness of God* (Ephesians 3:14-19).

I do not need the blessing of mere man or the titles he bestows. I need Him and Him alone. Man cannot give you the Holy Spirit. Man cannot fill you with His Holy Spirit. Only God knows our potential; only He knows what He has dreamed for us. We should not limit ourselves to what we think we can do or even what someone has told us we can do. The fullness of God dwells within. Because of that, we are easily capable of doing all He places in our hearts to do. There are those He sends to us, however, who will stand with us, understanding who we are, what we are called to do. In many instances, they too are called in a similar fashion.

Our problem is that those God brings to our side are not the "lovely ones" or those with influence that we want to be identified with.

This does not mean it will be effortless. He plants His own resolve within as we encounter the trials that test the word He gave us. He causes us to discover the greatness of His provision within and gives us the resolve we need to push through sometimes staggering opposition. Each road-block causes us to reaffirm our assignment. When difficulties cause our resolve to waver, they either strengthen us because we are certain of His calling, or these problems burn up a man-made vision that does not have the breath of God on it. These are not attacks of the enemy; these trials are gifts from our Lord to either make us stronger for the mission we are on or they redirect us from wood, hay, and stubble so we can truly find His plan for us. One thing is certain—where He leads, He far exceeds our expectations.

When Brokenness is dispatched to our side, her job is to turn our weaknesses into strengths, to increase our vision. There is no doubt that we are all much more than we have become. As the church Jesus is building and as individuals who are each part of that church, we are exponentially greater than the things we have done or the things we can imagine. Brokenness will open your eyes to see your potential, your possibilities, your power to become more than you have ever thought possible.

Now to Him who is able to do far more abundantly beyond all that we ask or think, according to the power that works within us, to Him be the glory

in the church and in Christ Jesus to all generations
forever and ever. Amen (Ephesians 3:20-21).

Do not be afraid of your dreams! Don't be afraid to watch what God is doing! You will undoubtedly discover things you can be a part of in His master plan for this planet. In the last analysis, responding to Him with a resounding *"Yes!"* will open the door of your heart to let Him be all He is through you. He uses all that He is when it suits His purposes at the moment. He can and will do anything through the one who lets Him. Everything He does molds His purposes so that the world can see Him and be a part of His heart's desire for humanity.

Our Lord is actively looking for God watchers. I know He is looking for folks just like you! I know who you are, for we have the same heart.

Epilogue

SEEING THE SONG

He put a new song in my mouth, a song of
praise to our God; many will see and fear
and will trust in the Lord (PSALM 40:3).

WHO SEES THE SONG?

THERE IS A SONG IN THE LAND THAT FEW ARE SINGING, EVEN fewer are hearing. But it is a Song that sets the heart dancing and pours hope into the soul. This Song is well worth listening for. It is well worth seeing. It is loud enough for all to hear, no matter who you are or what you have done. Yet it is soft enough to soothe the anguish of the mind and comfort the fears of the life you left so long ago. The Song erases the past and sets the course for the future. It sings forgiveness, wholeness, and destiny. It sings of life so abundant that there is never a verse of this Song that is repeated, so vast is the salvation which it describes. Yet the refrain of His Song is haunting, healing, refreshing, hopeful. Its unveiling will take an eternity to discover, yet but a moment to enter, to experience. It is seen in the lives of many who have heard its wonders and entered its possibilities. It gathers, heals, and restores what one would have never dreamed possible. The Song is free for the seeing, for the hearing, for the singing, for the experiencing.

The Song of which I sing is the Song of the Lord. It was sung long before the earth was created. It was brought to our awareness by the prophets who were the first in this dimension to hear it and sing its powerful melodies. It was fulfilled at the Resurrection of our Lord and is daily written on our hearts to announce the triumph of our King over all His enemies and ours.

Its joy is contagious and its fulfillment certain. God watchers the world over have joined the chorus of angels in the expression of this salvation in the Song to the nations. It is received with gratitude by the hungry and by nature that groans for the sons of God to live their calling to be the deliverers they were created to be and redeemed to become.

The Song is the reality of all that God has accomplished for humankind. It is the invitation for all to enter in His chorus that transcends time and space. Nothing can stop His Song. Nothing can stop those who dare sing it. For this Song *is* salvation. It *is* the great *"It is finished"* that echoed through every dimension of reality, shaking the very foundations of all that He made. The eternal chains of destructions could be heard clanging to the ground as Hope entered the stage and gave grace, mercy, and forgiveness to all who waited anxiously for His appearing with His glorious Song. Now, not only the angels sing this Song, not just the cloud of witnesses, but all who will lift their spirit heavenward to hear Him sing. To you, my Lord says:

> *"Shout for joy, O barren one, you who have borne no child; break forth into joyful shouting and cry aloud, you who have not travailed; for the sons of the desolate one will be more numerous than the sons of the married woman," says the Lord. "Enlarge the place of your tent; stretch out the curtains of your dwellings, spare not; lengthen your cords and strengthen your pegs. For you will spread abroad to the right and to the left. And your descendants will possess nations and will resettle the desolate cities. Fear not, for you will not be put to shame..."* (Isaiah 54:1-4).

Come! Sing with me!

ABOUT DON NORI, SR.

DON NORI SR., FOUNDER OF DESTINY IMAGE PUBLISHERS, has worked in the publishing industry and ministered internationally for more than thirty years, working with people of all races and nationalities. Don and his wife, Cathy, live at the foot of the Appalachian Mountains in south central Pennsylvania where they raised their five sons and now enjoy their daughters-in-law and their grandchildren. Don spends most of his time writing and ministering internationally.

Visit Don Nori's website for his itinerary, video blogs, and new books: www.donnorisr.com.

You may also view his YouTube videos at www.youtube.com/donnorisr, as well as viewing his daily posts and interacting with him on Facebook: https://www.facebook.com/donald.nori.

To contact him regarding a speaking engagement, e-mail him at: donnorisr@gmail.com